From Primates to Politicians

A journey from the political side of
animals to the animal side of politicians

Juan Manuel Muñoz

Wisdom
Editions
Minneapolis

Wisdom Editions

SECOND EDITION DECEMBER 2022

From Primates to Politicians

Copyright © 2020 by Juan Manuel Muñoz.

10 9 8 7 6 5 4 3 2

ISBN 978-1-960250-32-2

Cover and interior design: Gary Lindberg

Men judge generally more by the eye
than by the hand,
for everyone can see, but few can feel.
Everyone sees what you appear to be,
few really know what you are.

Nicolás Machiavelli

Table of Contents

From Primates
to Politicians

Wisdom
Editions
Minneapolis

Foreword

Could it be that there is a missing link between our politicians and the most animal aspects of human essence? It would be interesting to explore, and it might turn out that there is none, that they all in fact belong to the same species!

A patient once asked me, "How does an ophthalmologist view politics?" ... hmm ... interesting question. Doctors opining on politics is nothing new, but would the approach of a physician/political scientist be different? Perhaps the way reality is interpreted is the same, but the vantage point is distinct.

A few months ago, on a visit to Europe, a clerk in a bookstore told me that she had recently assisted a customer who was looking for a "book for not thinking." I don't think this book would comply with that request. *From Primates to Politicians* explores the very nature of human beings, our societies, our psychology and our evolutionary foundations. In some respects, it raises more questions than answers; in others, we may never have an answer; but in any case, the journey through who we are and how and why we organize ourselves is a delightful one.

I started this book with a review of various bibliographic sources following a surprising turn of events for many: the election of President Donald Trump in November 2016. It was a triumph that went against many predictions, involving numerous social phenomena, worthy of being studied to better answer questions such as: Who are we? How do we think? How do we behave as a species, and as a society?

Over the months I have been writing down ideas and organizing them little by little into paragraphs. All this has been happening amidst patients and between surgeries, and of course I have had to give up the little time left to a busy doctor to sit down and write late at night. I have had to sift through all sorts of material: scientific, journalistic, anecdotal, in short ... every possible source of knowledge has been welcomed, in order to explore the subject of primate behavior and its legacy in our societies, in search of the roots of human political and social behavior. Throughout the process, I have made efforts to avoid ideological, moralistic biases and to eliminate any gross prejudice.

Eliminating moral and ideological biases can produce uncomfortable reasoning for some readers but will hopefully serve to produce a freer way of thinking, or perhaps even a smile. If any of the approaches or arguments offend or contradict the views of any reader, I apologize. The content of this book has been gathered with love, always looking for truths based on solid arguments and evidence. Scientific thinking is part of my training, and I try to be loyal to it.

In the exercise of thinking, doubts arise that can be fun to share, or even interesting. They lead us to explore multiple disciplines, which can help us see human political evolution from different angles. My review includes material related to zoology, sociology, sociobiology, psychology and neuroscience, all mixed together and analyzed from the perspective of political science, which seeks a better understanding of human political behavior in varying circumstances.

In this book I have assembled intrinsic evolutionary and biological aspects of humans, which lead us to what I will call the "evolutionary theory of politics". It is structured - after analyzing a large volume of information - to share with you, so that together we can make an analysis of politics: an art that is understood and dominated by economic power and expert marketing manipulators able to turn the exchange of ideas into a struggle for sympathy within a "market" of voters.

It should be noted that throughout my review and analysis of the literature, I have researched information from sciences dominated by women, such as primatology, in order to contrast them with sciences dominated by men, such as political science, which are associated more with access to power and the eternal struggle for it.

I hope you enjoy the research and analysis presented here, in the same way that I had fun throughout all these months, looking for every little piece of what seems to be a dynamic, changing, and infinitely large puzzle.

I. Concept of primatology

Primates are mammals, descended from a common arboreal ancestor. Although many have adapted to different environments, most still live mainly in trees in tropical areas.

Primates include many species, such as monkeys and greater primates or apes from Asia and Africa. They live mainly in the equatorial areas of America, Africa and Asia. There are at least 496 recognized species, rising to 695 with the inclusion of sub-species. New species are constantly being described (103 since 1990, and 74 since 2000) [1]

Despite the great variability among primates, all retain the anatomical and functional characteristics of a common ancestor. For example, their brains are greater in proportion to total body weight when compared to other land mammals, and they are the only mammals with flat nails.[2]

---

[1] "Primates-SG - Who Are The Primates?" *Primate*. Accessed July 13, 2020. http://www.primate-sg.org/who_are_the_primates/.

[2] Napier, J.R., and Colin Peter Groves. "Primate." *Ency-*

Primates are characterized by binocular vision, the ability to grasp and the development of brain hemispheres. Laboratory observations show that the large primates possess skills and intelligence that have been broadly underestimated throughout history[3]. Binocular vision seems to have been an important factor in the expansion of brain structures and in the increase in brain size, throughout evolution.

The large size of primates' brains is associated with their great intelligence and makes them capable of solving problems or even using tools to defend themselves and to access food.[4]

There is vast evidence that humans are primates, given their genetic and physical similarities with apes. It is known that humans, chimpanzees, bonobos and gorillas have a common ancestor who lived 6 to 8 million years ago, and that the evolution of the human species developed entirely in the African continent. Between 15 and 20 species of primitive humans have been recognized, but there is no consensus as to which of them gave way to the appearance of man or which simply disappeared by natural selection.[5]

clopædia Britannica. Encyclopædia Britannica, Inc., April 5, 2020. https://www.britannica.com/animal/primate-mammal.

3   The Editors of Encyclopaedia Britannica. "Primatology." *Encyclopædia Britannica*. Encyclopædia Britannica, inc., November 6, 2016. https://www.britannica.com/science/primatology.

4   *MonkeyWorlds*. "Monkey Species." Monkey Facts and Information. Accessed July 13, 2020. http://www.monkey-worlds.com/monkey-species/.

5   "Introduction to Human Evolution." The Smithsonian

These similarities can be observed in studies such as those showing that human infants and baby monkeys process numbers similarly, which promises to lay the groundwork for understanding the evolutionary basis of more complex behaviors.

There is still heated debate about communication systems between nonhuman primates and the correct use of sentences, but in any case, communication between primates evokes the complexity of communication between humans.[6]

Seriously? Humans come from primates? Hmm ... Well, I'm sorry to inform you that, regardless of your creed, we won't be getting into that debate. True, there is the creationist proposal [789]. In fact, it took

Institution's Human Origins Program, January 16, 2019. http://humanorigins.si.edu/education/introduction-human-evolution.

6   [online] Available at: <http://www.iupui.edu/~mstd/a103/primate%20lecture%203.html> [Accessed 13 November 2017].

7   www.VantagePoint-BD.com, Vantage Point Business Development. Creation Versus Evolution. Accessed July 13, 2020. http://www.clarifyingchristianity.com/creation.shtml.

8   Menton, Dr. David. "Chapter 8: Did Humans Really Evolve from Apelike Creatures?" Answers in Genesis, February 25, 2010. https://answersingenesis.org/human-evolution/ape-man/did-humans-really-evolve-from-apelike-creatures/.

9   David E. Pratte, Light to My Path Publications. "Creation or Evolution: Which Does the Evidence Support?" Creation vs. Evolution | Origin of Man & Animals. Accessed July 13, 2020. https://www.gospelway.com/topics/god/creation_evolution.php.

Charles Darwin 20 years to break the silence around his observations on the evolution of species, and even after his publications, he avoided defending it in public [10]. In the end, he could not escape becoming a target of cartoonists and the mockery of many people.

However, like it or not, the theory of evolution tells us about the adaptation of living beings to changes in the environment, generation after generation. Currently, natural selection is one of the scientific theories supported by the greatest amount of scientific evidence, and the most widely accepted among scientists. In fact, it is backed by evidence from multiple disciplines such as genetics, molecular biology, paleontology, geology, comparative anatomy, comparative embryology, biogeography, microbiology and even radioisotope studies to determine the age of fossils [11][12]. If, despite the evidence, it still bothers you that we discuss the issue from an evolutionary point of view, I think it is time to close this book, go to the bookstore and ask for a book for not thinking.

So, diving into the topic that brings us here... What exactly *is* primatology? Well, according to the

10   "Charles Darwin: Evolution and the Story of Our Species." *BBC Teach*. BBC, November 20, 2019. http://www.bbc.co.uk/timelines/zq8gcdm.

11   Than, Ker. "What Is Darwin's Theory of Evolution?" LiveScience. Purch, February 27, 2018. https://www.live-science.com/474-controversy-evolution-works.html.

12.   BioLogos. "What Is the Evidence for Evolution? - Common-Questions." BioLogos. BioLogos, January 14, 2019. http://biologos.org/common-questions/scientific-evi-dence/evolution-evidence.

dictionary, primatology is simply the branch of zoology dedicated to the study of primates,[13] mainly other than Homo sapiens.[14]

But exactly what do they study? When we talk about primatology, we are referring to the discipline that carries out the scientific study of primates. This involves anatomy, anthropology, biology, medicine, psychology, veterinary medicine and zoology, among others. Those who study it do so seeking knowledge about living primates as well as extinct species (including some of our ancestors). They are studied in their natural habitat as well as in laboratories, with the goal of observing and analyzing how behaviors vary throughout evolution.

Where did the idea of studying monkeys come from? The answer is simple: primatology as an intellectual tradition emerged in the United States, Canada, Western Europe and Japan after the Second World War. Usually, primatologists are psychologists, anthropologists, and less commonly, biologists or zoologists. [15]You can also find studies of primatology in medicine, veterinary medicine and biomedical research.

Primatology has developed into two branches: Western primatology and Japanese primatology. The

---

13   "Primatologist." Dictionary.com. Dictionary.com. Accessed July 13, 2020. http://www.dictionary.com/browse/primatologist.
14   "Primatology." *Merriam-Webster*. Merriam-Webster. Accessed July 13, 2020. https://www.merriam-webster.com/dictionary/primatology.
15   "Take the Next Step to Becoming a Wildcat." *What is Primatology*? | Primate. Accessed July 13, 2020. http://www.cwu.edu/primate/what-primatology.

first studies of primates conducted in the West were biomedical in nature, but then expanded to include understanding their intelligence and mental prowess. Primatology involves different methods of studying primates, from field observations to controlled laboratory studies. Japanese primatology developed with greater emphasis on the social evolution of primates and argues that the study of primates can tell us about the evolutionary nature of human beings.[16]

Western primatology studies the common links between humans and primates, focused on understanding the evolutionary relatives closest to humans in order to increase our knowledge of our shared nature. Studies are usually controlled to avoid bias, even if this means replicating a social environment in captivity. We western humans perceive our attitudes in terms of good and bad actions, while primatology tries to understand human actions by understanding our behavior as primates.

Japanese primatology, on the other hand, developed in the animals' natural environment in the wild. Unlike Western primatology, the Japanese became more interested in the study of the social traits of the species, seeking a duality in human nature (the individual being versus the social being). The focus on social aspects made Japanese primatology a more

---

16"What Is Primatology?" *Journal of Primatology*: Primatology Journal: Define Primatology: Academic Room." What is primatology | Journal of primatology | Primatology journal | Define primatology | Academic Room. Accessed July 14, 2020. http://www.academicroom.com/topics/what-is-primatology.

subjective science than Western primatology, while at the same time allowing for better observation of the nature of everyone in natural conditions. According to Juichi Yamagiwa, Japanese primatology initiated its studies from the sociological perspective, when Kinji Imanishi began making observations in macaques with the aim of better understanding human societies. With this, a comparison was sought between human societies and primate societies. The first Japanese primatologists were convinced that the social behavior of primates responded to specific norms and the sociability of each species.

Over time, as primatology has matured as a discipline, it has advanced to taking more representative samples of all individuals of the studied groups in order to study them with equal interest and attention, and not only focus on the most powerful.

By 2001, it was estimated that 80% of the doctorates in primatology were awarded to women, causing it to be labeled a feminist science, with the biases that this may imply.

It should be noted that primatology is not an exact science. Like other scientific disciplines that unite objective and subjective aspects, the bio-social study of primatology implies complications and biases, so much so that primatology has even been used to search for arguments that justify socio-political agendas.

Regardless of which branch of primatology we are referring to, they all carry out studies that cross over into other academic disciplines, such as psychology, zoology, and biology. The sociobiology of the 80's and 90's brought primatology to anthropological studies and has been used by behavioral ecologists to form a reductionist view of behavior. Primate behaviors have shown evolutionary connections to humans, giving rise to theories about social and ecological factors that have influenced the evolution of different species. It has been interesting to study social intelligence, individual decisions, behavioral strategies and variants in populations of the same species and discover the presence of common goals and not just individual ones. The change in the size of the primate populations being studied has allowed us to investigate patterns of affinity, competition and reproduction. Social flexibility and complexity represent ancestral states of human evolution. Certainly, there are huge differences between humans and nonhuman primates, but the contribution that evolutionary comparison can give is valuable and significant.[17]

Due to the destruction of the primates' natural habitats, many species are likely to disappear in a not-so-distant future, and while many conservation efforts are being carried out, it is an arduous battle. Undoubtedly, this has led to a situation in which the main challenge for modern primatology - both Western and Japanese - is the conservation of the different species of monkeys and apes, a conservation that allows us to continue learning from them and, indirectly, about ourselves as human beings, part of an evolutionary chain.

So, have we learned anything interesting from monkeys and apes? Well, throughout evolution, the development of the capacity of hominids can be observed,

---

17   *Primatology as Anthropology*. Accessed July 14, 2020. http://www.anthropologiesproject.org/2011/08/primatology-as-anthropology.html.

towards abstract thinking and the use of symbols that have imbued individuals with a conscious notion of themselves. Barsalou even states that in evolution, a single pattern of brain development, maturation and learning experience has emerged, from prokaryotes to humans. Studies in macaques have reported that the circuit for conceptual knowledge in social situations is similar to the corresponding circuit for this purpose in humans. Learning in humans requires two attributes: flexibility and selection. This adaptability is provided by a modular structure in which organization of the modules is even predictable. The modular structure changes as the learning occurs. Among animal species, in general, despite the differences, there are nuclei, neuronal pathways and cerebellar functions, all relatively preserved from common ancestors.[18]

Primate studies have uncovered interesting aspects of different species of monkeys and apes. For example, Sumatran orangutans often make tools, even in the wild. They use leaves as toilet paper and large leaves as umbrellas. They also connect sticks to reach an object. In captivity, they can even surpass chimpanzees at manufacturing and using tools.

A study of primate archeology revealed that chimpanzees in West Africa have been able to pass on the technology of stone use to open seeds for many generations. Excavations carried out by evolutionary anthropologists in Côte d'Ivoire show stone artifacts

18. 2020. [online] Available at: <http://www.iupui.edu/~m-std/a103/primate%20lecture%203.html> [Accessed 14 July 2020].

made and used by primates over a period of 4,300 years, with a level of precision known only in humans. There are also reports of the use of stone tools by Capuchin monkeys in Brazil, and by macaques in Thailand.[19]

In macaques, it has been observed that techniques for feeding and caring for offspring are transmitted between members of a group. Even vocalization techniques seem to be learned and transmitted to the rest of the group. Today, young Japanese primatologists use artificially created feeding sites to study macaques in their natural habitat. Interestingly, it has been found that under conditions of abundance of food, some groups of macaques compete more fiercely with each other than others.

Among primates, there are different types of social structures:

- Polyamia (a male with multiple females) is seen in gorillas, pottos, spider monkeys and patas monkeys.

- Polyandria (a female with multiple males), is rare and is seen in marmosets and tamarins.

- Bisexual (mix of males and females), common, and can lead to the formation of friendships and consortiums (couples that last for days or months) between chimpanzees, bonobos, macaques, and some lemurs, Old World mon-

---

19   Barras, Colin. "Earth - Chimpanzees and Monkeys Have Entered the Stone Age." *BBC*. BBC, August 18, 2015. http://www.bbc.com/earth/story/20150818-chimps-living-in-the-stone-age.

keys such as savanna baboons, green monkeys, squirrel monkeys and some spider monkeys. The primates most closely related to humans are found in this group.

- Monogamy: in pairs (a male with a female), rare behavior usually seen in arboreal, territorial primates with minimal sexual dimorphism, and occurring in gibbons, indri lemurs, titi monkeys, pithecids, owl monkeys, and pottos.

- Solitary (single individuals), rare, and is observed in nocturnal prosimians such as aye-ayes, and lorisiformes.

Is there any benefit for primates living in groups? Apparently, yes. Groups enable sharing of food resources, finding partners and protection from predators, although competition for food and mates can lead to violence within the group.

The fact is that primatology allows us to make comparisons that even help us understand the evolutionary behavior of essential aspects including psychology, among many others. Thanks to these comparisons, it has been observed that humans have genetic expressions that probably give plasticity to our brains for more years, while in chimpanzees, the plasticity of their brain seems to be less than a year after birth.[20]

Human personalities, according to psychologists, have five dimensions: extroversion, consciousness,

---

20   "What's a Man?" *The Economist*. The Economist Newspaper. Accessed July 14, 2020. http://www.economist.com/node/21545972?zid=313.

neurosis, complacency and openness. Chimpanzees would seem to have six dimensions, three of them equal to humans: extroversion, complacency and openness; the dimension of "reactivity" is like the human dimension of "neurosis", but with some differences. The other two dimensions are: dominance and methodicalness.[21]

In short, the study of primates has been opening doors to a better understanding of how nature brought us to where we are today as a species. Perhaps at some point we will be able understand the more animal side of our politicians, by studying the more political side of other animals.

---

21 "Planet of the Apes." The Economist. The Economist Newspaper. Accessed July 14, 2020. http://www.economist.com/news/science-and-technology/21579438-chimpanzees-personas-seem-more-complex-peoples-planet-apes?zid=313.

II. Evolutionary trees

We know that humans and other primates, having proceeded from the same ancestor, have certain things in common. And obviously, we will look more like the species with which we share more recent ancestors. But why not take a closer look at evolutionary theory first?

In 1859, Charles Darwin's theory on the origin of species was published, putting poor Darwin into direct confrontation with creationism, the dominant way of thinking in his time. Darwin had to collect information on how humans evolved to explain the process. According to Darwin, only individuals with better adaptation to the environment survive and reproduce, while the weak die in a process known as natural selection. Darwin's ideas were subsequently applied to other fields of knowledge including administration, economics and sociology, eventually giving rise to theories such as "social Darwinism." Likewise, multiple disciplines have emerged that derive their basic theories from the theory of evolution. The political sciences have not been the exception, as evidenced by the emergence of evolutionary politics, which, of course, forms part of the subject matter of this book.

Evolution occurs through inheritable changes that become more common or scarce in a population based on natural selection, by which a certain characteristic benefits the survival of the population or facilitates reproduction. Evolution is widely validated by fossil records, embryology and comparative anatomy, and has served as the central principle that informs modern biology and explains the diversity of life on our planet.[22]

This gives rise to the big question of what exactly is meant by the term "inheritable changes". Well, to put it simply, all of an individual's biological information is organized into approximately 20,000 to 25,000 genes formed by hundreds to millions of nitrogenous bases of deoxyribonucleic acid (DNA). While most genes are the same among individuals of the same species, there are a few differences which give unique characteristics to each one. [23]From our genes, all the proteins that give rise to structures and move the different parts of our cells are formed, with mechanical actions coupled to chemical events. The movements resulting from these chemical processes enable the extraordinary capacities responsible for

22   "Evolution." *Science Daily*. Science Daily. Accessed July 14, 2020. https://www.sciencedaily.com/terms/evolution.htm.

23   "What Is a Gene? - *Genetics Home Reference - NIH*." U.S. National Library of Medicine. National Institutes of Health. Accessed July 14, 2020. https://ghr.nlm.nih.gov/primer/basics/gene.

the dynamic processes in living cells.[24]

When a cell reproduces, changes may occur in the nitrogen bases in the genes. These changes are called mutations, and when they occur in germ cells, they are passed down to subsequent generations, making the changes inheritable. These inheritable changes may represent evolutionary advantages for the next generation, but may also represent disadvantages, as in the case of hereditary diseases. Individuals with advantageous mutations, through evolution, are better equipped to survive or reproduce, causing the change in the DNA of a gene to spread in a population. Thus, the accumulation of mutations, generation after generation, shapes the natural evolution of a species.

The origin of primates dates back approximately 65 million years. From this point, more than 500 species originated throughout the planet.[25] The ancestors of primates (protoprimates) were more similar in appearance to rats (scientific name: Purgatorius) than to modern monkeys (there are those who jokingly say that when politicians act like "rats", they are simply recalling their origins).

Today, there are more than 260 species of primates which have appeared over more than 50 million years of evolution. It is not clearly understood how evolution

---

24   Alberts, Bruce. "Protein Function." *Molecular Biology of the Cell*. 4th edition. U.S. National Library of Medicine, January 1, 1970. https://www.ncbi.nlm.nih.gov/books/NBK26911/.

25   Gorillas-World. "Gorilla Evolution." *Gorilla Facts and Information*, February 1, 2017. http://www.gorillas-world.com/gorilla-evolution/.

produced ramifications in so many different directions.[26]

Primates are normally subdivided into three groups: prosimians, new world monkeys, and old-world monkeys and apes.[27]

Despite the notable differences between the different groups of primates, there are shared anatomical and functional characteristics which reflect the inheritance of a common ancestor.[28]

While prosimians are still found in the wild, they are limited to the island of Madagascar, some areas of Africa and Southeast Asia. Among them, we find the galagos (galagonidae), lorises (loridae), aye-ayes (daubentoniidae), dwarf lemurs and mouse lemurs (cheirogaleidae), lemurs (megaladapidae and lemuridae), indris, sifaka and wooly lemurs (indriidae), and the tarsiers (Tarsiidae).[29]

Prosimians are characterized by prominent snouts, laterally situated eyes and long tails.

Among the new world monkeys, there are several families which can be found in Central America,

---

26   MonkeyWorlds. "Monkey Species." *Monkey Facts and Information*. Accessed July 14, 2020. http://www.monkeyworlds.com/monkey-species/.

27   "Primate." ScienceDaily. *ScienceDaily*. Accessed July 14, 2020. https://www.sciencedaily.com/terms/primate.htm.

28   Napier, J.R., and Colin Peter Groves. "Primate." *Encyclopædia Britannica*. Encyclopædia Britannica, inc., April 5, 2020. https://www.britannica.com/animal/primate-mammal.

29   2020. Pixelteca.Com. 2020. http://www.pixelteca.com/biolog/primates/prosimios.html.

Mexico and South America. New world monkeys are descendants of African primates who colonized South America 40 million years ago. They are small to medium in size, with a well-developed prehensile tail. All except the howler monkey lack color vision. New world monkeys later migrated back to Africa across land bridges.[30]

Old world monkeys are more closely related to apes. The difference between monkeys and apes is that the former are smaller and usually have a tail. Apes, in contrast, have longer limbs with opposable thumbs.

The hominoid superfamily, or apes, appeared 25 million years ago, and corresponds to the genus Propliopithecus.

The gibbon was the first living primate to separate from the common evolutionary tree 18 million years ago. Despite this separation, it seems to be the primate that retains the closest resemblance to the common ancestor of all apes and humans.[31]

The family of apes includes gibbons, orangutans, gorillas, chimpanzees, bonobos, and of course, humans. Apes are smarter than monkeys and can learn signs, languages, handle tools, and solve problems.

30."Chimpanzee Evolution - Chimpanzee Facts and Information." n.d. http://www.chimpworlds.com/chimpanzee-evolution/.

31 "Ancestor of All Apes Might Not Be What Scientists Expected, New Fossil Shows." 2015. *Los Angeles Times*. October 29, 2015. http://www.latimes.com/science/sciencenow/la-sci-sn-ape-fossil-evolution-diverge-20151029-story.html.

The great apes are more threatened than we would expect. All species of great apes, except the mountain gorillas, show sustained decline in their populations. Their habitats are threatened by deforestation and slash farming. For this reason, good practice guides have been created to facilitate the understanding of the problem by researchers and conservationists.[32]

The orangutans branched out on the evolutionary tree approximately 14 million years ago. Currently, two species of orangutans have been identified: Pongo pygameus, on the island of Borneo, and Pongo abelii, on the island of Sumatra. They are the largest arboreal mammals and have the longest childhood among primates. Females begin to reproduce around age 16, and males acquire all their sexual characteristics between 20 and 30 years of age. [33]

Gorillas separated from the human evolutionary tree approximately 11 million years ago. At present, they are subdivided into gorillas from the east (Gorilla beringei) and from the west (Gorilla gorilla). The subspecies are separated by a great distance, so they have adapted to very different habitats. The two subspecies separated 2 million years ago and are geographically separated by the Congo River. Western gorillas have brown fur, including on their heads, while eastern or mountain gorillas have black fur but no fur

32   *Primates-SG - Great Apes of the World.* (n.d.). Www.Primate-Sg.Org. Retrieved March 29, 2020, from http://www.primate-sg.org/great_apes_in_the_world/

33   *Orangutan Biology.* (n.d.). Official Orangutan Foundation International Site. https://orangutan.org/orang-utan-facts/orangutan-biology/

on their heads. Mountain gorillas are the most studied subspecies. Although western gorillas share similar habitats in overlapping regions, there are no reports of competition between the two species.[34]

Chimpanzees, along with bonobos, are our closest living relatives. Their separation in the evolutionary tree seems to have occurred 5 to 8 million years ago. Chimpanzees divided into two subspecies, the common chimpanzee (Pan troglodytes) and pygmy bonobos or chimpanzees (Pan paniscus), 1 to 2 million years ago, following the formation of the Congo River, which creates a natural barrier that prevents mating between the two species. The chimpanzee is not an ancestor of humans and has undergone numerous changes that have facilitated the survival of both subspecies in their natural habitat.

Like us, chimpanzees can use stone tools, which might suggest that our common ancestor was the first to develop this technology. However, the use of stone tools by macaques in Thailand and Capuchin monkeys in Brazil suggests that different species of primates have each come to use stone tools on their own. The sophistication of objects manufactured by humans with stones is attributed to brain development, which resulted from the ability to control fire for cooking food and providing enough calories to maintain a larger brain.

Although chimpanzees do not control fire, they are able to recognize the benefits of cooking food, and this

---

34   *Primate Factsheets: Gorilla (Gorilla) Taxonomy, Morphology, & Ecology.* (2019). Wisc.Edu. http://pin.primate.wisc.edu/factsheets/entry/gorilla

has been proven repeatedly in different experiments. Everything would seem to indicate that primates have not yet reached the highest level of technology of which they are capable, but we do not know if they will be able to advance beyond the Stone Age,[35] mostly because of the threat we humans represent to their survival.

Before Darwin, Carl Linnaeus organized animals into groups according to their morphology. Because of their similar appearance, he placed Homo sapiens, chimpanzees, orangutans and gorillas in the order "Primates". Modern taxonomy (the description and classification of species), which is based on molecular aspects, has reinforced this relationship through DNA studies. A similarity of up to 99% has been found between Homo sapiens and chimpanzees. For comparative purposes, the primates closest to Homo sapiens are found in the Hominidae family, which includes the great apes.[36]

There is abundant scientific evidence of human evolution, thanks to the thousands of human fossils, tools, prints, paintings, and other clues that have been found, allowing us to study multiple physical and cultural aspects of the first species of humans, over 6 million years ago. From footprints, we can study the behavior of the first humans and compare them with

35   Barras, C. (2015). *Chimpanzees and monkeys have entered the Stone Age*. Bbc.Com. http://www.bbc.com/earth/story/20150818-chimps-living-in-the-stone-age
36   "What Is Primatology | *Journal of Primatology | Primatology Journal* | Define Primatology | Academic Room." n.d. Www.Academicroom.Com. http://www.academicroom.com/topics/what-is-primatology.

other primate species. The most recent advances in genetics provide us with a greater understanding of the similarities and differences between humans and other primates.[37]

Although the concept of human evolution is disturbing to many people, there are researchers who have reconciled their beliefs with the scientific evidence to contribute valuable knowledge about our origins as a species. To this day, there are those who deny the scientific evidence, whether for religious reasons, personal beliefs or simply because the topic seems too complex for them to understand.

The evolution of humans is often portrayed as the contrast between man and monkey. However, apes as a group cannot be studied or understood if the human species is excluded. For scientific purposes, humans are simply one more primate in the group, period. It is not worthwhile to try to understand our species as something supra-natural or as the center of the universe. An anthropocentric mentality only robs us of the possibility of learning about ourselves and understanding the relationship between our biology and politics.

Although humans may just be one more group of primates in the family tree, it is also true that we have our own characteristics which define us as a species, just as all other species of apes they have their own characteristics. The different species of primates should

37 Smithsonian's National Museum of Natural History. 2010. "Human Evolution Evidence." *The Smithsonian Institution's Human Origins Program*. March 1, 2010. http://humanorigins.si.edu/evidence.

not be understood as a series of changes "towards humanity" since humans themselves are simply one more species. The changes that the different species have undergone provide evolutionary advantages that allow each species a better chance of survival in its environment or greater reproductive opportunities.[38]

Paleoanthropology has given us the opportunity to learn more about the evolution of human species based on cultural, social and biological findings. The process of evolution involves naturally occurring biological changes to the DNA of cells that can be transmitted to subsequent generations within a species.[39]

According to Darwin, we should not expect the common ancestor of humans and chimpanzees to display perfectly intermediate characteristics between the species to which it gave rise. Rather, it could have had characteristics that tended more toward any one of the evolutionary branches that arose from it. The skeletal characteristics of the first hominids, regarding their skull and hips, suggest that they were more terrestrial than arboreal, and usually bipedal, unlike chimpanzees. Each Homo species had unique characteristics. Therefore, they cannot be considered as a linear sequence towards today's humans. We know that as Homo evolved, they

---

38   "The Emergence of Humans." n.d. Evolution.Berkeley.Edu. http://evolution.berkeley.edu/evolibrary/article/evograms_07.

39   Smithsonian's National Museum of Natural History. 2010. "Introduction to Human Evolution." *The Smithsonian Institution's Human Origins Program*. March 1, 2010. http://humanorigins.si.edu/education/introduction-human-evolution.

began to manufacture tools that required complex manipulation; all this accompanied by the increase in cranial capacity and a more erect posture.

There are people like Dr. Rick Pottos who suggest that the evolution of humans had a lot to do with climate change and climate instability. For example, bipedalism is an advantage in climate conditions of drought and tree shortage. Similarly, sudden and drastic changes in the weather may have given rise to the selection of individuals with greater cranial capacity. This increase in cranial capacity accelerated in the space of just 4 million years, particularly in the last 800,000 years, which coincided with the period of greatest climate instability. It is possible that this increase in brain size allowed for solving abstract problems and planning. It would not be far-fetched to suggest that severe climate changes have extinguished many species of hominids in our recent evolutionary tree, giving way to the development of our species as the predominant one. Hominin behavior itself may have developed in response to climate stress since fossils have been found in different and changing habitats.[40]

For years, researchers have tried to devise hypotheses about human proclivities regarding political and social behavior. Then, in 1987, Richard Wrangham stated that if humans, gorillas, chimpanzees and bonobos

---

40   Smithsonian's National Museum of Natural History. 2010. "Climate Effects on Human Evolution." *The Smithsonian Institution's Human Origins Program*. March 2010. http://humanorigins.si.edu/research/climate-and-human-evolution/climate-effects-human-evolution.

share a common ancestor, we should be able to identify a set of human behaviors shared with our nonhuman relatives which would correspond to the behavior of our common ancestor.[41]

41. "Political Primates." n.d. Greater Good. http://greater-good.berkeley.edu/article/item/political_primates

III. Power relations in animal societies

If we define politics as power relationships within a society, we could say that politics is practiced by all living beings on the planet. We know that life depends on resources such as oxygen, sexual partners, nutrients, water, etc., to fulfill the function of being born, growing, and reproducing. Power relationships arise because some of these resources are limited in a given habitat.[42] From bacteria, which compete in places with more nutrients or better conditions for reproduction, to plants, which compete by sending out roots to obtain nutrients from the earth, or trees, that compete in the forests for direct access to sunlight. Seeing it from a slightly more romantic perspective, even flowers compete with their beauty to attract bees and achieve pollination, which

---

42   "Interaction between Different Species | Ecology." 2016. *Biology Discussion*. September 16, 2016. http://www. biologydiscussion.com/biodiversity/species/interaction-be-tween-different-species-ecology/51886.

allows them to reproduce. It seems that competition for resources is intrinsic to life itself.

When the great philosopher Aristotle used the term in his work "Politics" in the 5th century BCE, affirming that man is a political animal, he revealed the deeply anthropocentric perception prevalent in his time. We could say that a somewhat different concept was understood by the word "politics." At that time, he used the word derived from "polis" to refer to human societies, the way of governing, and the organization of its citizens. However, societies are not exclusive to human beings. The organization of power is not exclusive to our species, much less the organization among individuals.

Humans simply respond to natural characteristics common to other living beings, characteristics that even determine power relations in different species, as can be seen in the food chain of any ecosystem. From its inception, the term "politics" had an anthropocentric, humanistic origin, and at no time was it considered that human beings might be nothing more than another group within the animal kingdom. It is a distortion of reality to try to understand animals through the lens of human societies. We are better off trying to understand human societies through the study of animal societies and their evolution. All animals, plants, protozoa and such are political to some extent, in the sense that they exercise power over each other in an eternal struggle to access life-sustaining resources.

More than superior primates, humans are, first and foremost, animals, so it is worth analyzing the general biosocial behavior of different species of living beings to better understand ourselves. Branches of knowledge such as sociobiology - a branch of biology which states that social behaviors are a product of evolution - try to explain such behaviors within this context. In the study of human beings, sociobiology shares much with Darwinian anthropology, human behavioral ecology and evolutionary psychology. It draws on ethnology, anthropology, evolution, zoology, archeology and population genetics, among other sciences. Sociobiology starts from the premise that social and individual behaviors are greatly affected by the heritage of natural selection. It is a way of understanding how behavior has been changing, in the same way that physical traits have changed. This allows us to understand the evolutionary advantages that different social behaviors represent, each in their own context.

The behavior of animals is based on hereditary structural, psychological and physiological aspects, which are proximate causes. In addition, there are past events that have also shaped behavior, and we will call these ultimate causes. Both the proximate causes and ultimate causes unfold in such a way as to increase the likelihood that the responses to a given circumstance are beneficial for the individual.[43]

Nature seems to know about economics. It always tends towards thrift, following the principle of least effort. We find this principle everywhere, in physical

---

43 "Animal Social Behaviour - The How and Why of Social Behaviour." n.d. *Encyclopedia Britannica*. https://www.britannica.com/topic/animal-social-behaviour/The-how-and-why-of-social-behaviour#ref1044812.

reactions, the movement of the stars, enzymatic reactions, thermodynamics, and, of course, animal behavior. For most actions in nature, the most likely path seems to be the one that involves the lowest energy consumption and the lowest possible resource consumption, in general. Economizing energy and resources seems to be the guiding principle behind both physical evolution and behavior patterns in animal societies.

In nature, there are all kinds of interactions between individuals within a species and between different species. This includes a variety of social interactions, which can be classified as mutualism (mutual benefit), altruism (one sacrifices to benefit another), selfishness (one benefits at the expense of another), and resentment (one hurts another and both tend to be harmed).

In *mutualism*, there is a relationship of mutual benefit between species that is straightforward, since it is in itself an evolutionary advantage.[44]

In *altruism* there is voluntary sacrifice of one to benefit another. It is rare outside of humans and apes and requires mutual trust between the parties for the agreement to be maintained. It has been shown in animals that even subtle deceptions can break the altruistic agreement. Altruism is the most complex form of social interaction, so much so that the game theory has been applied to try to understand the altruistic agreement between unrelated individuals. A solution to maintaining

---

44   *2017. [online] Available at: <http://www.bbc.co.uk/ schools/gcsebitesize/science/ocr_gateway_pre_2011/environment/2_compete_or_die1.shtml> [Accessed 14 November 2017].*

an altruistic agreement is reciprocal altruism. This seems beneficial in animal societies, but only when there is a mechanism to punish individuals who receive benefit without reciprocation, even if by a third party. The truth is that despite its complexity, altruism represents an evolutionary advantage in itself, in a certain group within a society, since collaboration maximizes its benefits and generates greater reproduction.

Interactions resulting from *selfishness* are seen, for example, in parasitism, in which one of the species benefits while the other is harmed. Another example of a selfish relationship is commensalism, in which one organism benefits while the other is not benefitted or harmed. In both cases, there is only evolutionary advantage for the beneficiary.

While no one usually benefits from *resentment,* it does seem to work when the affected party obtains some subsequent benefit. The best example of this type of relationship is that of predators and their prey. Typically, in predation, there is an attack by the strongest on the weakest, for example a frog on an insect, or an eagle on a mouse. Predation relationships are complex between the two species involved.

The grouping together of living beings can produce new behaviors that offset the cost of association. Animals are grouped around some benefit, either with beneficial interactions or without further interaction between them. In the first case, the cost of maintaining the beneficial grouping should not be exceeded by the benefits received from it. Moreover, the benefits of forming coalitions are like those of gathering into groups. Ostensibly, animals join for two main reasons: food and defense. Among the social behaviors we can observe are *nepotism*, the formation of *alliances* or groups, and *communication* systems, which increase the benefits and defense of the group. In groups of animals that congregate for defense, the alarm signal is considered an altruistic behavior, since it places the individual who sounds the alarm at risk of attack by the predator.

We could say that in power relations in nature, species are subject to stress which can lead to extinction or adaptation. The delimitation of a territory reduces competition and combat. The tendency to monopolize territories varies between species, and even in the same species, over time. Biologists argue that it becomes viable when the benefit of restricting access exceeds the cost of defense, following the principle of least effort. When the resources are of very good quality, the competition can become so intense that it makes exclusivity impossible or simply makes the defense too expensive.

Domain interactions are behaviors within or between social groups to establish a hierarchy for access to resources. Dominant individuals tend to be more aggressive and successful at winning in competitive interactions with other individuals. The domain can be obtained by direct aggression, or by mutual agreement, in which the dominant individual assumes greater benefit. Game theory is applicable in correlating the cost of fighting for resources with the potential benefits. The establishment of hierarchies in the domain can be advantageous because it reduces the frequency of damage caused by dangerous fights. Individuals at lower levels of the hierarchy have only a couple of options: change groups or go it alone. Striking out alone means losing the benefits of being in the group and migrating to another group implies the challenge of finding one that allows you to achieve a higher level in the hierarchy. The opportunities for young animals to rise in the hierarchy improve with what they learn as subordinates.

Nepotism in the upper levels of hierarchy favors the permanence of younger relatives in the group, where young subordinates often develop tactics to take advantage of status.

It is important to mention that communication is critical in social interactions, since it is necessary for assembling, for domain interactions and for competition interactions.

Regarding dominance: it produces a stability that brings benefits to all parties, since dominance between species or within the same species prevents the fights, cost, damage and instability that can occur. There are those who argue that dominant individuals do not force the rest to follow them; rather, their physical advantage and their influence with the opposite sex makes it easier for them to establish their place within the group. Similarly, knowledge also foments leadership, as it can allow the group to obtain more resources for everyone. Dominance is common in species such as primates and wolves but can be seen even in insects. It is common for these dominant individuals to take leadership roles, to coordinate the group to achieve collective action in situations of conflicts of interest, while maintaining internal peace within society. In groups of ants, those who know the path to food guide others. It is also interesting to note that among bees, only an elite 5% of the colony participate in the decision of where the group will go. In some species, the leader's decisions are absolute (despotism), and in others, any individual can act to coordinate (democracy).[45]

It has been observed that under despotic leadership, without clear benefit to the subordinate, submission only remains effective until the subordinate finds the opportunity to do battle in conditions where he has a chance to win. In this case, the dominant member can respond with more violence to maintain the asymmetry of power in the relationship, or it may yield some access to resources to the subordinate, to maintain peace and stability.[46]

Now, if animal societies seem to follow the principle of least effort, what can be said about struggles and conflicts? Well, an example is a study conducted by biologists at UCLA, in which they concluded that the main cause of fighting between dragonflies and other species of animals which cross their path, is related to access to females in a certain area .[47] It seems that animals fight when it is "worthwhile" to fight; that is,

---

45 King, Andrew J., Dominic D.P. Johnson, and Mark Van Vugt. 2009. "The Origins and Evolution of Leadership." *Current Biology* 19 (19): R911–16. https://doi.org/10.1016/j.cub.2009.07.027.
46 "Social Dominance Explained Part I." n.d. Psychology Today. https://www.psychologytoday.com/blog/games-primates-play/201203/social-dominance-explained-part-i.
47 "Why Do Animals Fight Members of Other Species?" n.d. UCLA. http://newsroom.ucla.edu/releases/why-do-animals-fight-members-of-other-species.

when the potential benefit exceeds the risk and cost of the fight.

The behaviors related to violence, dominance and struggle that are observed in animals could surprise you. For example, ants can organize in large numbers to attack termite colonies, in what might resemble outright war. Another startling example is that there are ants that take other species of ants as slaves. Now, remember that nature knows about economy! In cases in which the benefit of coexistence outweighs the benefit of conflict, even species that may be enemies can live together, as is occasionally the case with ants and termites[48]. It is worth mentioning that the association between predator and potential prey is rare and is usually not long-lasting.[49]

On the other hand, animals with genetic and neurological conditions that involve high levels of fear tend to be less aggressive, and stressful and dangerous situations can affect them more dramatically. Animals with a tendency to feel more fear may die of a heart attack under stressful conditions in which they perceive great danger.[50]

---

48   "Do Animals Go to War?" 2016. National Geographic News. January 30, 2016. http://news.nationalgeographic. com/2016/01/160130-animals-insects-ants-war-chimpanzees-science/.
49   Venkataraman, Vivek V., Jeffrey T. Kerby, Nga Nguyen, Zelealem Tefera Ashenafi, and Peter J. Fashing. 2015. "Solitary Ethiopian Wolves Increase Predation Success on Rodents When among Grazing Gelada Monkey Herds." *Journal of Mammalogy* 96 (1): 129–37. https://doi. org/10.1093/jmammal/gyu013.
50   Grandin, Temple. 2005. "'Our Inner Ape': Hey, We're the Monkeys." *The New York Times*, October 9, 2005,

Now, remember that associations do not have to be exclusively between individuals of the same species. We can observe associations between different species, only these are going to depend on their diet, social system, and phylogenetic distance (distance between species). The diet of the species is important because nutrition involves practically all aspects of animal life, including its organization in societies. It has been observed that the distribution of food in a given space can limit the nutritional balance of each individual, particularly when there are few nutrients in a large area. Social interactions serve above all to regulate individuals in conditions of scarcity, rather than abundance.[51]

A complicated example of interaction between species is the association between primates and non-primates. They are usually commensal in nature and found in complex environmental conditions.

Of the interactions between humans and other species, such as dogs, there are still many mysteries. One attempt to unravel such mysteries has been the study of the association between wolves and baboons in East Africa. The wolves learn to live among the baboons and ignore their young, which could be

sec. Books. http://www.nytimes.com/2005/10/09/books/review/our-inner-ape-hey-hey-were-the-monkeys.html.
51   Lihoreau, Mathieu, Michael A. Charleston, Alistair M. Senior, Fiona J. Clissold, David Raubenheimer, Stephen J. Simpson, and Jerome Buhl. 2017. "Collective Foraging in Spatially Complex Nutritional Environments." *Philosophical Transactions of the Royal Society of London. Series B, Biological Sciences* 372 (1727). https://doi.org/10.1098/rstb.2016.0238.

potential prey. The baboons, on the other hand, show complete confidence that they will not be attacked by the wolves. Now, the question is: Will there be any benefit from such interaction? The mechanism is not clear, but it has been observed that wolves have a higher success rate in hunting rodents when they are among baboons than when they are alone.[52] It is important to mention that in a fight between a wolf and a baboon, neither is usually able to easily defeat the other. Fights are long, incurring painful wounds without achieving any benefit or triumph[53], and would be unlikely as they do not comply with the principle of least effort.

Thinking about the relationship between wolves and baboons leads us to examine our relationship as a species with dogs, and to consider aspects of domestication, such as whether punishment works as a way to change a behavior or establish a relationship of clear dominance of one species over another. Well, just as we can learn about ourselves from animals, we can learn about animals from our species. A pediatric study showed that hitting children makes them more aggressive and difficult to discipline as they grow. In the case of dogs, the increase in their aggressiveness is related to the type of punishment. Like children, dogs

52   Holmes, Bob. n.d. "Monkeys' Cosy Alliance with Wolves Looks like Domestication." New Scientist. https://www.newscientist.com/article/dn27675-monkeys-cosy-alliance-with-wolves-looks-like-domestication/.
53   "Buhari vs. PDP: The Dog and the Baboon Parable, By Dr. Aliyu U. Tilde - Premium Times Nigeria." 2012. May 20, 2012. http://www.premiumtimesng.com/opinion/5195-buhari_vs_pdp_the_dog_and_the_baboon.html.

often develop an aggression clearly directed against the person who applies the punishment.[54] In the end, positive reinforcement of desired behaviors has shown to be more effective and sustainable and implies more efficiency in energy consumption.

So, what can be said about the behavior of biological systems? Does it make a difference when there is coordination among them, or not? The answer, of course, is that it does make a difference. Living beings interacting in a society can behave like a larger living being, in which each individual is a part of the resulting organism. Unlike the interactions between atoms and molecules, biological systems can move more complexly. Single biological microorganisms usually have simple movements; however, in animals, including humans, the cohesion of individual actions can lead to a greater impact on a larger scale. The scale of the impact will depend on the spatial range, duration, momentum and energy of the behavior. The main mechanism in biological systems, to maintain a coordinated behavior, is the exercise of control by an individual (leader) over the behavior of others. The greater the likelihood of individual success, the greater the level of collective complexity, as the levels of interaction increase among surviving individuals.[55] Groups that act in coordination can also

---

54   "Is Punishment an Effective Way to Change the Behavior of Dogs?" n.d. Psychology Today. https://www.psychologytoday.com/blog/canine-corner/201205/is-punishment-effective-way-change-the-behavior-dogs.
55   "Complexity Rising: From Human Beings to Human Civilization, a Complexity Profile." n.d. New England Com-

confuse a predator by giving the impression that they are a single animal, larger than the grouped individuals. When predators work together, they can also confuse a group of prey, separating an individual from the group and making it easier to capture.

Social interactions, either within the same species or between different species, can cause collective behaviors to arise. Collective behaviors refer to social events and processes that occur as behavioral externalizations which go beyond the social structure, laws and institutions. Collective behaviors occur in a disorganized and spontaneous way (for example, a euphoric and impulsive crowd in a stadium, clashes with the police, vandalism, etc.) and are not exclusive to humans. It has been observed in many forms of animal societies, including insects.

While it is interesting to talk about interactions between different species and between individuals of the same species, in a book about animals and politics, a question that is increasingly gaining relevance in the public debate and that cannot be overlooked is: Are homosexual interactions natural? Objectively, the answer is yes. Natural homosexual activity has been observed in at least 10% of living animal species. Although homosexual encounters are common in the animal kingdom, the puzzle remains of why they occur, and if there is any advantage in them. In the case of the tropical fish "Mexican Poecilia", males participate in homosexual activity in the presence of female voyeurs,

plex Systems Institute. http://necsi.edu/projects/yaneer/ Civilization.html.

increasing the visibility of those males that otherwise would not have a chance to attract females. [56]Likewise, homosexual or bisexual behaviors have been observed in beetles, flamingos, sheep, fruit bats, dolphins, orangutans, and macaques, among many others, perhaps as a form of control for obtaining resources or for the formation of alliances that impact reproductive success.[57]

Now, getting back to the matter at hand: Can it be said that societies have a geometric distribution? Are there patterns that can be identified, that are repeated in nature? That's a good question. Without a doubt, the sphere and the spiral are patterns that are repeated in nature. The spherical shape seems to be universal and is the product of external forces such as surface tension and gravity, as well as forces of internal cohesion, such as chemical bonds. Acting together, these forces cause objects to take on a form that allows them to pack the largest volume with the smallest external surface. There are forms such as our galaxy that are derived from spheres which are flattened by centrifugal force [58]. Matter encounters a force that stresses it and forces

56 "Behavior Brief." n.d. The Scientist Magazine®. http://www.the-scientist.com/?articles.view/article-No/33990/title/Behavior-Brief/.

57 "Homosexual Activity Among Animals Stirs Debate." 2004. Science. July 23, 2004. http://news.national-geographic.com/news/2004/07/0722_040722_gayanimal.html.

58 "Omnibus." n.d. Www.Haydenplanetarium. Org. http://www.haydenplanetarium.org/tyson/read/1997/03/01/on-being-round.

it to acquire the smallest possible surface, frequently resulting in spheroidal forms. Does the same happen in animal societies? Well, at least where human beings are concerned, it has been suggested that modern society is pyramidal, with resources at the apex of the pyramid.[59] But is there another possible way to understand the organization of societies? Are there stressors that surround them and put up resistance to their growth? Apparently, yes. Constant interaction between species represents a continuous stress for them, in an ecosystem with limited resources. But do mathematical or geometric rules apply to social structures? It could be thought that animal societies take on forms derived from the sphere, or from spheres that interact with or are connected to each other, as more efficient forms. Animal societies and plant groups often cluster around resources and minimize their exposure to external stressors such as predators, shortages, or other environmental threats. We see it in oases, and it is no accident that our cities tend to take a circular shape, which can be deformed by external stress factors (such as the coast, mountains, lakes, etc.). Is it possible for a society to take on a form solely for efficiency's sake? The answer is yes. In fact, all biological systems follow the path that requires the least expenditure of energy to achieve an outcome. The concept of social efficiency refers to the point where there is maximum social benefit with the lowest social

---

59   *2017. [online] Available at: <https://mamatucci. wordpress.com/2012/01/21/the-spherical-society-will-re- place-the-pyramid-one/> [Accessed 14 November 2017].*

cost.[60] It would make sense to expect a social structure to naturally tend toward the most efficient form. It is also true that there are proportions and numbers that are repeated in nature in different geometric figures, such as leaves, petals, the thickness of tree branches, snail shells, hurricanes, galaxies, and even the DNA in our cells[61]. This could lead us to ask: Is there an equation that allows us to better understand the distribution and structure of animal societies? There may be, but the subject goes beyond the scope of this book.

60   Pettinger, Tejvan. n.d. "Social Efficiency." Economics Help. http://www.economicshelp.org/blog/2393/economics/social-efficiency/.
61   Manual, Byline. 2013. "What Is the Golden Ratio?" Live Science. Live Science. June 24, 2013. https://www.livescience.com/37704-phi-golden-ratio.html.

IV. Power relations in the tree of Homo sapiens

In the previous chapter, we reviewed certain factors that affect the social behaviors of living beings, and the different patterns of interaction between individuals within a species and between different species. To understand human behavior a little better, we can take a closer look at primates, our nearest relatives. We need to understand that despite the evolution of each species over millions of years, we retain characteristics of our common ancestor as an intimate part of our biology and psychology.

Primate species, including humans, are very sociable, which makes time spent in captivity difficult and tedious. Primates can establish interesting and complex hierarchical structures in their social groups.[62] Like humans, the high sociability of nonhuman primates

---

62.MonkeyWorlds. n.d. "Monkey Species - Monkey Facts and Information." http://www.monkeyworlds.com/monkey-species/.

forces them to have to deal with leaders, power games, disappointments, adultery, and regret[63]. Within social structures, primates can acquire behaviors, make alliances, and even organize political strategies with a level of complexity that can easily lead to bloody conflicts.[64]

While rebellious behaviors are punished within an established social order, there are times when it may be deemed worthwhile to face the risk of punishment in exchange for the chance to ascend within the social hierarchy, which can result in better access to valuable resources or simply favor reproduction. Groups benefit when the punishment is meted out by a single individual (the dominant or alpha member), since imposing punishment has a cost, which is assumed by this individual[65]. It has been observed, for example, that in many species, the female is the authoritarian, and the young inherit the social role of the mother. Theory of mind states that leadership is nothing more than the product of asymmetric information management among

63   "What Is Primatology | Journal of Primatology | Primatology Journal | Define Primatology | Academic Room." n.d. Www.Academicroom.Com. http://www.academicroom.com/topics/what-is-primatology.

64   "UCLA Faculty Voice: What Monkeys Can Teach Us about Politics." n.d. UCLA. http://newsroom.ucla.edu/stories/ucla-faculty-voice-what-monkeys-can-teach-us-about-politics.

65   King, Andrew J., Dominic D.P. Johnson, and Mark Van Vugt. 2009. "The Origins and Evolution of Leadership." *Current Biology* 19 (19): R911–16. https://doi.org/10.1016/j.cub.2009.07.027.

individuals in a group, where an individual who is able to understand what others know, want, and do, obtains social advantages that lead an improved status within the social hierarchical structure.

As we can see, there are multiple similarities between human behaviors and those of other primates. It is important to mention that despite the similarities in primate and human leadership, the size of the human brain and the large size of human groups makes the leader selection environment unique. The intelligence of humans has led us to levels of complexity unmatched by any other species, although our essence is maintained from one generation to the next and our origins continue to predominate in the development of our behavior.

Communication is a key element that increases the level of complexity of the social structure. For example, in nonhuman primates, an abundance of vocal and visual cues are given by the leader to guide the group. Primates have been observed to use a wide variety of sounds for this purpose. It is interesting to note that there are experts who think that groups can develop their own variation of "language" which they teach each other, with differences between geographical regions (like different languages in humans). In fact, it has been found that this pattern is repeated in different species.

On the other hand, if communication serves as a force for social cohesion, population size may be a factor that leads to its disintegration. The size of the population can exceed the cognitive ability of its individuals, leading to a schism. Thus, the increase in a primate population requires time for socialization to keep the group together. Sustained growth requires a lot of socialization time to maintain cohesion within the group, and that is where language plays an important role. Language increases the efficiency of the socialization time necessary to maintain the unity of a large group and allows for simultaneous socialization with several individuals.

Dominance in a primate community can lead to a greater capacity for reproduction or a monopoly on food. This is why individuals try to increase their power, in relation to others, through the manipulation of social relationships. And while social relationships incorporate dimensions of affiliation, they also imply competition for food, mates and other desirable resources. Among primates there are variations in the frequency of aggression, directionality of aggression, tolerance to individuals of greater hierarchy and asymmetry in relationships. However, not all aggressions result in access to resources, and some asymmetries of power may be the product of unilateral submission, not aggression.

If we pay attention to the species closest to humans in the evolutionary tree, we can see that among the behaviors shared by bonobos, chimpanzees, gorillas and humans is the tendency to live in groups, and to attack members of the same species. Chimpanzees and gorillas have proven to be extremely politically ambitious, to the point of forming coalitions to challenge the dominance of alpha males and eliminate them from the community. Similarly, primatologist Frans de Waal found that chimpanzee females can come together to achieve partial control over alpha males. Likewise, female bonobos form small coalitions which can increase the power of subordinate females to the point of putting them on par with dominant males in competitive situations. Rebellious behavior is present in the three species closest to man (gorillas, chimpanzees and bonobos), suggesting that the common ancestor did not like to be dominated and created coalitions to upset the power of the alphas, or of individuals who could occupy an alpha position.[66]

Next, let's look at some aspects of the power relationships that characterize the modern primate species closest to humans.

Chimpanzees

The social behavior of chimpanzees is mainly influenced by the scarcity of natural predators, their high efficiency for feeding, the amount of resources they have to defend themselves, and their high probability of success in getting a partner (since they are much more promiscuous than humans). Chimpanzees are grouped into large communities in which subgroups or parties are formed. These parties within a community are unpredictable and changing. The size of a party increases when food availability increases or there is a fertile female present. Males remain in the same community for a lifetime, while females migrate as teenagers, at age 14, in a transition that can take up to two years.[67] Nishida reported that

66   "Political Primates." n.d. Greater Good. http://greatergood.berkeley.edu/article/item/political_primates.
67   "Primate Factsheets: Chimpanzee (Pan Troglodytes) Behavior." 2019. Wisc.Edu. 2019. http://pin.primate.wisc.edu/factsheets/entry/chimpanzee/behav.

chimpanzees organize into communities, that males from different communities never get together or mix, and that males from different communities can engage in lethal battles. On the other hand, females are adopted and integrated into a new family group.[68]

Cooperation within communities seems to be one of the main evolutionary advantages of chimpanzees. Both inter-community interactions and intra-community politics seem to be the result, in large part, of kinship relationships between males. Inter-community interactions can be seen in the attacks carried out by groups of males in cooperative patrol parties, while intra-community interactions are dominated by cooperation between males to maintain dominance, hunt, and share meat.

Meat is valuable as a source of protein, but it also has social importance: it is used like paper money to make and maintain alliances. Usually the meat is shared with reciprocity, and not randomly (a kind of reciprocal altruism takes place). The members of the group appear to interact socially by sharing food to obtain favors from other members of the group.[69]

Chimpanzees have a hierarchy of dominance. In the hierarchical order, both males and females can hold high positions, although adult males tend to place themselves above females. Chimpanzees are aggressive and even engage in open combat,

---

68 "Bonobo ('Pygmy Chimpanzee') Sex and Society." n.d. Www.Primates.Com. https://www.primates.com/ bonobos/bonobosexsoc.html.

69 2017. [online] Available at: <http://sciencecases.lib. buffalo.edu/cs/files/chimpanzees.pdf> [Accessed 14 November 2017].

especially if they feel that someone from another group is invading their territory. Males tend to take control of the chimpanzee community in which they live to the point of forming alliances to overthrow the dominant male. When a male is defeated, he usually remains within the same group.

There is an interesting level of sophistication among chimpanzees in their struggle for power; brute force does not seem to be the only factor. Primatologist Frans de Waal noted that the size and strength of chimpanzees is not a good predictor of group dominance. It seems that the ability to socialize, and even diplomacy, are much more important traits.[70]

On the other hand, gestures of reconciliation have also been observed among chimpanzees after a fight, such as a hug or a kiss. Apparently, acts of reconciliation represent an advantage within a species where conflicts can easily arise between members of a community.

Similarly, experiments have shown that chimpanzees are good negotiators, to the point of having a good sense of whether an agreement is fair. They do not act purely from a selfish perspective, which has led scientists to conclude that a sense of fairness and justice was already present in the common ancestor of humans and chimpanzees before evolution separated the two species 7 million years ago .[71]

---

70   WIRED Staff. 2010. "The Psychology of Power." WIRED. *WIRED*. August 14, 2010. https://www.wired.com/2010/08/the-psychology-of-power/.
71   "Behavior Brief." n.d. The Scientist Magazine®. http://www.the-scientist.com/?articles.view/article-No/33990/title/Behavior-Brief/.

Chimpanzees have a sense of territory and of control of resources within a given territory. They are even able to carry out deliberate attacks on neighboring communities to extend the territory under their control. In fact, a 10-year study in Kibale National Park in Uganda found that conflicts over territories had left a toll of 18 dead or injured chimpanzees. The conflicts were carried out in a manner comparable to that of a guerrilla attack, rather than open war. Apparently, the term "war" is inappropriate when referring to conflicts in non-human species[72], and something as senseless as a total war (defined by the British encyclopedia as a conflict in which the opponents are willing to make any sacrifice in lives or resources in order to obtain a complete victory[73]) may be one of the most characteristic behaviors of the human species.

While chimpanzees may kill members of other groups, lethal attacks on members of their own group are not as common. However, power struggles between chimpanzees can lead to high levels of violence and be very bloody. An example of this is found in the account published by the New Scientist magazine in 2017, of a group of West African chimpanzees that attacked an adult male of their own group with sticks and stones. After beating him to death, they ate the flesh of the

---

[72]   "Do Animals Go to War?" National Geographic. National Geographic Society, January 25, 2018. http://news.nationalgeographic.com/2016/01/160130-animals-in-sects-ants-war-chimpanzees-science/.
[73]   "Total War | Military." 2019. In *Encyclopædia Britannica*. https://www.britannica.com/topic/total-war.

corpse. Between chimpanzee coalitions within the same group, there is a constant tension that moves between two extremes: cooperation and conflict. This tension increases when the density of males within the group increases, as was the case with the group mentioned in the publication.[74]

Another example of clashes between chimpanzees was the conflict in Gombe National Park in Tanzania. In 1974, a struggle arose among a group of chimpanzees that had grown up together and then parted ways, unleashing a conflict that lasted for years. During the fighting, not even the oldest members were respected. The event was comparable to a genocide. Despite this type of behavior, De Waal, in his book "Our Inner Ape", tells us that apes can learn peaceful behaviors and internalize them to continue practicing them within their group.

Attacks on humans by chimpanzees in captivity are somewhat frequent, although in their wild state they seem rather to fear humans. This suggests that chimpanzees in captivity perceive their physical strength to be superior to that of humans, which in fact it is: they are five times stronger than a man. An example of this type of attack occurred in 2009, when a chimpanzee nearly killed a woman in Connecticut, United States. Chimpanzee males are more aggressive than females, and violence is part of their common behavior. Mutilations of the face,

---

74   Whyte, Chelsea. n.d. "Chimps Beat up, Murder and Then Cannibalise Their Former Tyrant." New Scientist. https://www.newscientist.com/article/2119677-chimps-beat-up-murder-and-then-cannibalise-their-former-tyrant.

limbs, even testicles have been seen. Usually chimps in captivity end up in a cage, sooner or later, due to their violent temperament.[75]

Bonobos

Bonobos, also known as "pygmy chimpanzees," appear to have undergone fewer evolutionary changes over the past eight million years than humans or chimpanzees, meaning that they might be more akin to our common ancestor.

They are quite different from chimpanzees, despite their physical resemblance. Bonobos live in peaceful communities, where sexual activity is the preferred way to solve stressful problems. In fact, bonobos are often compared to a group of promiscuous "hippies" (with the 60's motto of "make love and not war").

While chimpanzee communities seem to be governed entirely by testosterone, with male domination clearly established in a vertical hierarchy, bonobos live in matriarchies. Chimpanzees practice violence broadly and frequently, while bonobos are not able to distinguish between a friendly caress and a sexual act. And while chimpanzees kill each other (in fact, infanticide is the leading cause of chimpanzee death, both in their habitat and in zoos), bonobos tend to feel more fear. The latter became evident during the bombing of Munich in World War II, when all the zoos' bonobos died of heart attacks, while all the chimpanzees survived.[76]

---

75   Harmon, Katherine. n.d. "Why Would a Chimpanzee Attack a Human?" *Scientific American*. https://www. scientificamerican.com/article/why-would-a-chimpanzee-at/.
76   Grandin, Temple. 2005. "'Our Inner Ape': Hey,

Among chimpanzees, behaviors that are common in humans are observed, such as cooperative hunting, food sharing, the use of tools, the exercise of political power and even war. These behaviors, however, have not been observed in bonobos. Chimpanzees sometimes demonstrate their strength dramatically, throwing stones and breaking branches, causing others to quickly get out of their way. Bonobos are less expressive, simply dragging a few branches here and there. You could say that they are more of the "easy-going" type.

Gorillas

Gorillas are subdivided into lowland gorillas and highland gorillas. Due to terrain and habitat conditions, most social observations of gorillas have been done in the western lowlands.

Dominant male gorillas are also called silverbacks. Gorillas move in minimum groups of two individuals (usually a silverback male and a female), unless it is a solitary male. The maximum number in a group can exceed 20 individuals in mountain gorillas but does not usually exceed 17 to 20 individuals in western lowland gorillas.

Usually, the females migrate from their natal group to another group, while the males remain in their natal group or set out on their own. Young males remain subordinate to the silverbacks but can take their place if one dies. Solitary males, on the other hand, have the option of enticing females to leave

We're the Monkeys." *The New York Times*, October 9, 2005, sec. Books. http://www.nytimes.com/2005/10/09/books/review/our-inner-ape-hey-hey-were-the-monkeys.html.

their group and starting a new group as a silverback. Relationships between male gorillas are poor, with high competition for females. Young males can form all-male groups in which they are more sociable, until the group disintegrates when they reach adulthood. There is evidence that Western lowland gorillas can live in groups in which there is an adult male, several young males and non-reproductive females.

Females can migrate in the company of another female to share a solitary male. Among gorillas of the eastern mountains, when there is only one male in the group, the females disperse upon its death. Among western lowland gorillas, however, when the silverback dies, the group stays together.

Like chimpanzees, gorillas also practice violence within their own species. Infanticides are reported in all subspecies of gorillas. In mountain gorillas, aggressive behavior is common but usually not intense, nor does it lead to significant injuries. Among female gorillas, there may be aggressive encounters due to competition for the male, who intervenes to stop the fight. Similarly, the silverback male intervenes when there is a young gorilla being attacked by individuals at a higher level of dominance.

It is worth mentioning that despite the stereotype created by King Kong, the dominance of silverback gorillas is not absolute. There is evidence that half of gorilla infants are not fathered by the dominant silverback male but by younger males, who are willing to risk discovery and attack for a chance to mate.[77]

---

77   "Primate Factsheets: Gorilla (Gorilla) Behavior." 2019. Wisc.Edu. 2019. http://pin.primate.wisc.edu/fact-sheets/entry/gorilla/behav.

Orangutans

Male orangutans often live alone, while females move about with their young. Sometimes groups of several adult males and females can form for a few days, weeks or months after mating. Individual females occupy a territory that partially overlaps with that of other females, and with a more extensive territory corresponding to that of the male, with whom they will mate. Such overlap allows social interaction between orangutans. Usually females remain in the same area when they mature, while males migrate to areas of other females upon reaching adulthood.

Orangutans can congregate in parties to feed themselves and to mobilize in search of food. Feeding clusters occur where there are fruit trees with abundant food and include male and female residents of the area as well as non-residents. The abundance of fruit decreases competition between them and allows them to look for partners.

While adolescent orangutans move in small groups, like gorillas, their behavior changes once they reach adulthood. Encounters between adult males are characterized by fights or competitions. The dominant male in an area is usually the one with the best physical condition and largest size.

Among females there are aggressive reactions when they meet, as they prefer adult males. However, there is evidence that, like gorillas, half of the offspring are not fathered by the dominant males in a territory. In the case of orangutans, young males have been known to take females by force.[78]

---

78   "Primate Factsheets: Orangutan (Pongo) Behavior." 2009. Wisc.Edu. 2009. http://pin.primate.wisc.edu/fact-

Macaques

Itani Kawai observed that macaques have a social structure based on small subgroups composed of males and females. He also noted that the groups are usually like each other.

Among macaques, males usually leave their natal group to join another group with different genetic characteristics. Studies have revealed that all males seek a dominant status level within the group, and that the losers leave the group to become solitary males. It is curious to note that the dominance of a male does not determine his reproductive success. Selection by a female, however, can determine his success in becoming a dominant male.

Juichi Yamagiwa observed in his studies that there are two ways in which females can become dominant: by being the daughter of a dominant female, or through the dominance of the eldest daughter over younger sisters.

As socio-ecology predicts, intense competition between groups can foster social bonds and nepotism.

While there are many curious facts about modern primates, what about our extinct relatives? Is there data on power behaviors among our ancestors and related extinct species? The answer appears to be a resounding yes, although the study of fossil remains is difficult and often subjective.

The image of the hunter in control of the terrain may be easier for us to understand in view of our current situation, but it is not the origin of our species.

sheets/entry/orangutan/behav.

Australopithecus afarensis, an ancestor of modern humans, was small and terrestrial. The study of his limbs seems to indicate that he spent most of his time trying to avoid becoming the food of other mammals. Although popular culture has absorbed the image of the killer ape, it is not supported by archaeological finds. At this time, the hominids were still shy scavengers who lived mostly in peace.

The start of meat consumption and the use of tools as weapons, two million years ago, seems to mark an increase in violence between groups. The risk of attacks among humans skyrocketed even more around a million years ago, with the invention of long-range weapons. There is evidence of cuts in the skull with damage to the eyes in Homo erectus remains. Human groups had occasional encounters which could become bloody, especially when dealing with territorial dominance.[79]

The oldest evidence of war between humans comes from the Nataruk massacre, which occurred 10,000 years ago in what seems to have been a violent confrontation between nomadic hunter-gatherer groups. Archaeological remains found in Kenya chronicled the death of 27 members of a tribe, including eight women and six children. They were apparently assassinated, as evidenced by crushed skulls and bodies injured by stone arrowheads. Some bore signs of having had their limbs tied. At the time of the massacre, the place was

---

79   March 2006, Heather Whipps 16. n.d. "Peace or War? How Early Humans Behaved." Livescience.Com. http://www.livescience.com/640-peace-war-early-humans-behaved.html.

rich in water and food, so it could have been an ideal place for a band of humans to establish themselves. This discovery attests to the intentional death of a group of humans, without burial of the dead, and gives us an idea of what relationships between different bands might have been like, in conflict. This type of behavior was continued in agricultural societies, as part of life in relationships between settlements. According to some, extreme violence in disputes between groups was more the rule than the exception. Evolutionary biology shows that humans have compassionate and supportive characteristics, but at the same time aggressive attitudes that easily reach lethality.[80]

Both the observations of the great apes and the evidence regarding our own origins lead us to conclude that certain parallels can be found between human populations and populations of other primates, or even of other living beings, in general. Some of these similarities will be discussed in the next chapter.

---

80   Kennedy, Maev. 2016. "Stone-Age Massacre Offers Earliest Evidence of Human Warfare." *The Guardian*, January 20, 2016, sec. Science. https://www.theguardian.com/science/2016/jan/20/stone-age-massacre-offers-earliest-evidence-human-warfare-kenya.

V. Comparing human and animal societies

In order to talk about the similarities and differences between human societies and those of other primate species (or any other animal), we need to understand that both hierarchies and levels of power are universally understood to be the levels of access or proximity to resources within a group. Usually, this refers to resources such as food, access to mating, or any other aspect that facilitates survival and/or reproduction.

In the case of humans, our intelligence, as well as the characteristics of our communication through language, make the behavior of any group of humans highly complex. Hence, a virtuous cycle has formed between intelligence and socialization, causing us to be increasingly intelligent while creating progressively more complex societies. This notion is supported by comparative studies of primates, which have demonstrated that socialization has been crucial to the enlargement of the human brain.

There have been consequences as human societies follow the path to complexity, such as the distortion of the concept of access to resources. This concept was first altered using bartering, and then by the appearance of money. In both cases, the goal is to facilitate access to resources necessary for survival. Any intermediate mechanism becomes a resource in itself, to meet the basic needs of modern living.

In fact, human societies have become so large, changeable and complex that more and more neural connections are needed to deal with them. This also means that politics remains an art which we are far from being able to decipher,[81] since mathematically it handles a number of variables that grow faster than our ability to understand them.

There are multiple disciplines that seek to compare behaviors between species, including humans. And as with studies of comparative anatomy, behaviors can also be compared in terms of the social and political structures of different groups within a single species, or of different species.

According to sociobiologists, the behavior of both human and non-human species can be explained as a product of natural selection and should be understood as such. They argue that behaviors are the result of the pressures on a given species throughout its history.

---

81   September 2016, Adam Hadhazy 29. n.d. "Life's Extremes: Democrat vs. Republican." Livescience.Com. http://www.livescience.com/17534-life-extremes-democrat-republican.html.

Primatology, like sociobiology, is an amalgam of objective and subjective sciences with social implications as well as biases, making it the subject of much criticism. In this regard, Western primatology has tried to focus on controlling the studies to minimize their subjectivity. Japanese primatology, however, has continued to try to adhere to the nature of what is studied.

Primatology serves to support the study of the biological and psychological aspects of nonhuman primates, and then seeks common links between humans and primates. The interaction between primatology and sociobiology examines the evolutionary process of primate behavior and analyzes what this process says about the human mind.[82]

Comparative primatology studies provide anthropologists with clues to human mechanical functioning, enabling them, for example, to better analyze and understand evolution. Primates have undergone evolutionary processes to adapt to different forms of life, some of them even like those of humans five million years ago. The cognitive abilities and sensitivities of large nonhuman primates may reflect the characteristics of humans that lived between 5 and 2 million years ago, of which we have no major clues to facilitate their study.[83] On the other hand, anthropology can incorporate new study patterns in which it is possible

82   "What Is Primatology | Journal of Primatology | Primatology Journal | Define Primatology | Academic Room." n.d. Www.Academicroom.Com. http://www.academicroom.com/topics/what-is-primatology.
83   "Primatology | Anthropology." n.d. Encyclopedia Britannica. https://www.britannica.com/science/primatology.

to relate the social and cognitive capacities of human beings with the behavior of primates.[84]

Another science that draws on the comparison between humans and primates is evolutionary psychology, which attempts to explain the basis of behavioral evolution through the study of different neural mechanisms.

Human behaviors are full of traces of our ancestors, that we embody all manner of ancient instincts around conservation and hunting. The common traits we share with other species can be found in every little aspect of life. It is curious that we came from an arboreal ancestor who sought refuge from predators in the highest treetops, and that to this day, in our "civilized" metropolis, the apartments on the top floors of our buildings are still the most valuable.

Another example of commonality can be found in the predictions obtained by computational models, which show that the behavior of a society led by a small group of informed individuals (as is usually the case, described in elite theory) is exactly the same as the predictions given for the coordinated behavior of animals such as fish and birds. In fact, if we are going to talk about leadership, it seems to have its origin in the need for coordination. Even in a group of two individuals, it is seen that one tends to move before the other, and thus leadership begins to emerge. According to game theory, the more similar the benefit, the easier it is for the two individuals to coordinate.[85]

---

84   Ryan Anderson. n.d. "Primatology as Anthropology." http://www.anthropologiesproject.org/2011/08/prima-tology-as-anthropology.html.

85   King, Andrew J., Dominic D.P. Johnson, and Mark

Human societies, like all other animal societies, cluster around the most valuable resources. This pattern can be observed even at basic levels of cellular organization. Numerical cell growth requires the influx of resources (vessels that carry oxygen and nutrients), while the most important cells receive more resources (vessels with oxygen and nutrients) through multiple pathways (the heart or the human brain, for example).

Every grouping around resources would seem to be based on two major determiners of behavior: leadership and synergy. It comes as no surprise that the synergy achieved through the coordinated movement of living beings in their environment can be observed in human societies as a product of discipline and compliance with norms and laws.

So why aren't actions always coordinated? There are times when actions are not only not coordinated, but even anarchic. Have you observed what happens when you attack a row of ants? In humans, there are collective reactions to events which are known as "collective behaviors." Some sociologists believe that in crowds, human behavior reverts to animal emotions as a general characteristic. Crowds induce people to lose their ability to think rationally.

Now, if we are going to compare humans with an animal, why not start with our cousins, the great apes? They are so like us that they use sophisticated mechanisms of social behavior to form and break alliances, including

Van Vugt. 2009. "The Origins and Evolution of Leadership." *Current Biology* 19 (19): R911–16. https://doi.org/10.1016/j.cub.2009.07.027.

altruism, deception and disappointment. In the same way as humans, primates are very social, and deal with intrigue, power games, reigns, and collective emotions.

It has been found that the frequency of the use of deception in a species is directly proportional to the average volume of the animal's cerebral cortex, and the great apes appear to make the most use of deception as a tactic to influence individuals around them. For primates, there seems to be no concept of dishonesty; they simply experience behaviors that give them the desired results.[86]

According to Frans de Waal in his book "The Bonobo and the Atheist", human morality has a lot in common with ape behavior and seems more characteristic of evolution than of divine imposition. Moral concepts are part of social behavior, and apes, like humans, have behavioral pillars of reciprocity and justice, on the one hand, and of empathy and compassion, on the other. It has been observed that chimpanzees are familiar the concept of ownership and have a clear concept of hierarchy. Like humans, apes experience gratitude and deal with the concept of "revenge." Social concern, as a higher degree of morality, is understood by apes, but in a more rudimentary way than in humans. Apes will intervene in fights to avoid serious consequences and understand the social benefits of reconciliation.

The question of commitments based on moral principles in human societies would seem antagonistic to the Darwinian struggle for survival. The evolutionary

---

86   Muir, H. (n.d.). *Sneakiest primates have biggest brains*. New Scientist. https://www.newscientist.com/article/dn6090-sneakiest-primates-have-biggest-brains/

explanation would be that moral principles are dynamic and take the form that most benefits and best guarantees the survival of the individual and of society. Otherwise, society would become extinct in the hands of the environment, or of other societies competing for the same resources.

Hence, the existence of a universal morality or wholly correct pattern of behavior is not to be expected. Everything seems to depend on the circumstances, so much so that certain facts cause us to question the purity of human acts of altruism. For example, wealthy retirees receive more visits from each of their children when they have more than one heir. Donations of goods and money to civic and religious organizations are another example since they are often greater when they are more visible. The latter may be related to the moral and social incentive that a donation entails; the individual may think that by making a public demonstration of altruism, he will be better viewed to occupy a position of power within society. Demonstrations of altruism may change when there is less probability of recompense or when selfishness has a good chance of going unpunished (as economist Steven Levitt mentions in his book *Super Freakonomics*).

Human envy also seems to have deep roots in the nature of primates. Proof of this is that capuchin monkeys have been observed to rebel when one individual receives a reward perceived as more valuable than that received by the rest of the group. [87]That's right!

---

87   Fisher, D. (n.d.). *Primate Economics*. Forbes. Retrieved March 30, 2020, from https://www.forbes.com/2006/02/11/monkey-economics-money_cz_df_money06_0214monkeys.html

Think of yourself as a capuchin monkey every time you remember how jealous you were when your mother gave your brother the reward, and not you.

Like humans, apes form small groups where cooperation is essential. Understanding the needs, intentions and temperaments of the other members of the group is crucial to attaining a position of power. Primates who know what others think and act accordingly, gain social advantage, take the lead and rise in their hierarchical status within the group.

Thus, for example, among capuchins, the decision to follow a leader lies in the accumulated knowledge that the leader has about each member of the group and their behavior in past situations.[88]

It can be said, then, that leadership is a characteristic that we humans share with many other species. In fact, an evolutionary approach to the study of leadership has been proposed. In humans, as in animals, the likelihood of an individual taking the lead to coordinate a group will depend on their motivation, temperament, dominance, and knowledge. Leadership can even be observed in certain species of fish in which the most determined individuals tend to take the lead while the shy ones tend to facilitate the leadership of others. That difference in temperaments is crucial to ensure coordination. Dominance in human beings is translated in terms of "social status." Leadership seems

---

[88]   *UCLA faculty voice: What monkeys can teach us about politics.* (n.d.). UCLA. http://newsroom.ucla.edu/stories/ucla-faculty-voice-what-monkeys-can-teach-us-about-politics

to be a solution for achieving the collective action and coordination necessary to have a greater impact on the environment in favor of the group.

Hierarchy systems in human societies, as in social animal species, give few options to individuals at lower levels, who often face only two choices: change groups or go it alone. This natural phenomenon allows us to clearly understand world migration patterns. Basically, migration will depend on the possibility of attaining more resources of better quality, or simply reaching a higher level of hierarchy than in the society of origin.

Ah! That explains everything! Migrants behave like animals! True, but make no mistake: We are *all* animals and we *all* behave like animals, even the xenophobes. Capuchin monkeys, like humans, are highly xenophobic, seeing other groups as enemies, and nothing unites a group better than a common enemy. A common enemy can cause internal conflicts within the group to be forgotten. It is no accident, for example, that, historically, every time there is an independence movement in a country as large and diverse as China, tensions arise with some neighboring country. Nor is it by chance that dictators with controversial and divisive personalities resort to nationalist rhetoric to win popular support.

The funny thing is that while cooperation suits us, the distribution of power seems always to be uneven. Social asymmetry would appear to be the cause of conflicts at all levels.

An example is seen in the observations made by Zuckerman in 1932. In these studies, it was found that male baboons killed each other in captivity, reinforcing the idea of competition between males to ensure dominance and access to the harem of females. Nevertheless, this type of behavior varies greatly among the different species of primates, including humans.

Another example of a power struggle that offers a clue to the evolutionary dynamics of our own species can be seen in the different species of dragonflies that compete for access to females. It comes as no surprise, then, that there is genetic evidence of interbreeding between Neanderthals and modern humans, which may have led to competition for females to the point of the Neanderthals' extinction.[89]

Fights using "weapons" can be observed in primates; warring clans use objects to injure each other and will fight to the death.

From all this, we can see a dark side, full of violence and death, intrinsic to our own genes. But would we be able to live in big cities if we were a cannibalistic, aggressive and purely violent species? While it is true that we are primates, we must remember that we also have our own characteristics as a species. Curiously, and contrary to the stereotype that was formed at some point, the first humans lived in groups of hunters and gatherers within a fairly egalitarian social structure, far removed from the groups of bonobos, chimpanzees and gorillas led by aggressive alpha males.[90]

89. "Why Do Animals Fight Members of Other Species?" n.d. UCLA. http://newsroom.ucla.edu/releases/why-do-animals-fight-members-of-other-species.
90. "Political Primates." n.d. Greater Good. http://greater-good.berkeley.edu/article/item/political_primates.

Like any other living being - or animal, for that matter, humans respond to incentives. In nature, instinct causes animals to seek out resources such as food and mating, for which there are clear economic, moral and social incentives. Indirectly, many of the incentives identified by humans are nothing more than products of the distortion of our basic animal needs (but between you and me, I still have my doubts about the evolutionary motivation for shopping). Now, is there any human who does not respond to incentives such as food or reproduction? Apparently, our response to incentives is so strong that the only way to achieve behavioral changes is through immediate incentives and disincentives. So much so, that there are experts who claim that if an incentive is not perceived in the short term, it is better to assume that there will be no change in attitude.

One thing is becoming clear: Machiavelli was at least partly right. The end *can* justify the means, even if the means is frowned upon by society. We are always hearing about corruption, to the point that the United Nations agreed to a convention against corruption. But what is corruption? Where did it come from? The explanation seems quite simple.

Corruption simply consists of giving or receiving money (or any other material good) in exchange for favors or social or political influence. Corruption is, to put it quite simply, comparable to chimpanzee behavior. Chimpanzees share meat or distribute it inside or outside the group for the sole purpose of obtaining favors. The size of the influence sought should be proportional to the size of the piece of meat, and the goal is usually to consolidate alliances to challenge power or maintain the status quo. As we can see, if we resemble capuchin monkeys when we are envious, some politicians and businessmen resemble chimpanzees when they receive or give bribes.

Humans, like the rest of the animal kingdom, are constantly searching for resources of all kinds. The more valuable or scarce the resource, the more intense the search and the willingness to take greater risks. To try to maintain order and avoid violence among individuals, society imposes economic, moral and social sanctions. But in addition to being sanctioned, there is another factor that plays an important role: the probability of being sanctioned. It is precisely this last aspect that causes greater corruption in some countries. However severe the sanction may be, if the probability of being sanctioned for breaking the social rules is very low, it may be worth the risk to obtain a valuable or scarce resource. In other words, we can say that practically the only thing that stops the universalization of corruption in our societies is the certainty of punishment and the fear that people may feel about violating the norms. To make matters worse, we might add that the acquisition of a valuable resource (such as stealing hundreds of millions of dollars from the state coffers) can place an individual in an advantageous situation of power (he can hire more and better lawyers), adding a further perverse incentive to commit crimes. In the end, all of us who have lived in developing countries know that no matter how civilized Nordic Europeans or Americans may seem, all they need is to feel the lack of certain punishment in order for uncontrolled corruption to become part of their daily lives.

Let's pause here for a moment: Can you imagine how terrible it is that someone is always watching absolutely everything you do, and can send you to a punishment that can last forever? I have no doubt about how valuable religions are, and their great importance in moderating individual behaviors within society. Even if we believe religion to be superstition, it is known that superstition has nothing to do with intelligence in humans, and is very positive for humans when there is a placebo effect (when a substance, object or action does not really have any curative effect, but the individual is led to believe that it will)[91]. It can be said that in one form or another, religion has accompanied us over tens of thousands of years as another evolutionary advantage.

The question here is, what about other animals? Do they also have something like religion, or superstitions? Well, the answer is yes. In fact, in animals, the development of superstition from a conditioned response has been observed. For example, birds can be taught that when they practice certain movements, food appears. In humans, on the other hand, superstition has been shown in experiments to improve the performance and accuracy of the individual in activities that require a lot of skill. However, it can also be harmful when it prolongs attempts to win at games of chance or to change an irreversible situation, such as trying to retain a partner.[92]

---

91   Albert, Sarah. n.d. "The Psychology of Superstition." WebMD. http://www.webmd.com/mental-health/features/psychology-of-superstition#2.

92   September 2013, Marc Lallanilla 13. n.d. "Fri-

Now, returning to our core theme: to better understand the complex social interactions between intelligent beings such as ourselves and our primate cousins, we need only remember the famous study carried out at Yale University with capuchin monkeys. The monkeys were given coins to use in a manner like the way humans use money. To the surprise of the researchers, capuchins appear to have very clear concepts of economics. It was found that monkeys changed their patterns of currency use (consumption) when there were changes in "prices." The study also found that when a monkey works and the benefits are distributed unevenly, it stops working. The monkeys, like trade unionists, seem to have the need to compare what they receive to what their peers receive. Similarly, they need to exchange goods with other monkeys, and feel that they receive a reward proportional to the work they do. Capuchins also tend take risks that can improve their chances of obtaining greater benefit.

If we compare the behaviors of different primates, we find that they are similar, but for different reasons. What one species does by instinct can even be learned by another species.

Capuchin monkeys trained to use the equivalent of money follow the laws of the market. They consume more products when they receive more at the same price. They even display the same type of irrational behavior as human beings about gambling. Surprisingly, monkeys

day the 13th: Why Humans Are So Superstitious." Live-science.Com. http://www.livescience.com/39566-fri-day-the-13th-superstitions.html.

can understand that not only can money be exchanged for food, but that it also gives the indirect ability to obtain other benefits. In the study, it was observed that the exchange of coins led to their exchange for sex, in a similar way to prostitution as practiced in human groups. Robberies and thefts among monkeys were also observed. And like many humans, monkeys placed no value on savings, even though it could reap them greater benefits later.[93]

If the capuchins were surprising, the macaques are not far behind. A study with macaques showed that a third of the macaques were willing to subject their partners to an electric current to receive a double ration of food in return. The majority (two thirds) of the macaques showed empathy. It was even found that there were "spiritual" macaques, or, more aptly, good-hearted macaques. In a few cases, the latter even chose to go hungry rather than subject their partners to the electric current. Those subjected to electrical current were less likely to subject their peers to electrical current as well (which makes me think that we should require our politicians to live in poverty before giving them access to power). Empathy seems to be fundamental to any species that cares for its offspring and is thought to be dependent not only on the development of the right

---

93   "How Scientists Taught Monkeys the Concept of Money. Not Long after, the First Prostitute Monkey Appeared." 2011. ZME Science. July 7, 2011. http://www.zmescience.com/research/how-scientists-tught-monkeys-the-concept-of-money-not-long-after-the-first-prostitute-monkey-appeared/.

amygdala, but also on previous experiences and on direct contact, even with other species. The pre-frontal region of the right hemisphere also participates in the emotional process, for example, in the detection of facial expressions and pain signals in other individuals, in addition to fulfilling a biological function particularly suited to the emotional recognition of a mother[94] (we will talk about neurological studies and functions later in this book).

Speaking of studies and experiments: there are experiments that occur outside the control of researchers, in which it is enough that we simply sit back and watch what happens. In one such study, the males grouped together under an alpha male in a well-defined hierarchical structure. The objective was to fight over territory to acquire more power in a larger geographical area. Some females joined the group, leading to polygamy. This is not surprising, since it can be found in any group of chimpanzees. The surprising thing is that this structure corresponds to the testimonies of ex-combatants who belonged to certain guerrilla groups in South America.[95] It has been reported that within a guerrilla group in Colombia, for example, free sex is practiced without stable unions, but under conditions of careful control by the commanders. Sexual interactions

---

94   "Neuropolitics.Org - Neuropolitics Resources and Information." n.d. Www.Neuropolitics.Org. http://www.neuropolitics.org/Conservative-Left-Brain-Liberal-Right-Brain.htm.
95   "Bonobo ('Pygmy Chimpanzee') Sex and Society." n.d. Www.Primates.Com. https://www.primates.com/bonobos/bonobosexsoc.html.

seem to be a form of exchange of favors within a power structure, in which women give sex in exchange for protection, better food, alcohol, medical care and the possibility of leaving their children in the care of their families. Hence, there is more sexual interaction with the commanders. The girls have been prepared for sexual activity since their entry into the guerrillas, many at around 12 years of age. This same group has boasted of practicing gender equity; however, women have never been known to occupy the group's upper ranks.[96]

Of course, it is difficult to talk about comparing behaviors between species without including aspects related to sexuality. It is interesting to note that, like humans, bonobos have sex outside the female's heat period. A point of controversy is why women do not go into heat to ensure receptivity at the precise time of ovulation. The truth is that bonobos are highly promiscuous, and despite behaviors developed by our species, there are scientists who claim that humans are not monogamous by nature. Monogamous mammals tend to defend an exclusive territory, have infrequent sexual activity, are intolerant of other adults of the same sex, their young leave the group, and they do not create social networks. Humans, however, share territory, have sexual activity with extreme variability, form groups with adults of the same sex for various purposes, their

96   Krystalli, Roxanne. n.d. "Why Free Love in the FARC Isn't so Free. (You Wouldn't Know It from Reading the New York Times.)." Washington Post. https://www.washington-post.com/news/monkey-cage/wp/2016/03/24/women-in-the-farc-have-had-a-mixed-experience-you-wouldnt-know-that-from-the-new-york-times/?utm_term=.c14d0bd99986.

offspring have varying patterns of residence, and they create elaborate social networks. Even in societies where monogamy is the ideal, most individuals do not practice it.[97]

Though it seems hard to believe, the study of animal societies allows us to understand so many things that might seem exclusive to our species... If you thought that sex merely for pleasure was uniquely human, what about having a pet? Well, I can tell you that baboons steal wolf cubs and take them to their group, where the two species will coexist. Coexistence between baboons and wolves has been observed in East Africa. The wolves live amid the baboons and ignore their young as potential food. This type of behavior gives us a clear idea of how human domestication of the first wolves (which would later be our current dogs) must have taken place.[98]

---

97   "Primate Behavior." 2020. Iupui.Edu. 2020. http://www.iupui.edu/~mstd/a103/primate%20lecture%203.html.
98   Holmes, Bob. n.d. "Monkeys' Cosy Alliance with Wolves Looks like Domestication." New Scientist. https://www.newscientist.com/article/dn27675-monkeys-cosy-alli-ance-with-wolves-looks-like-domestication/.

VI. Evolution of human societies

So, we have seen that humans are a primate species sharing much in common with the rest of the animal kingdom and even more in common with our cousins, the apes. But we also have our own characteristics as a species, the product of natural selection through the multiple environmental adversities we have faced throughout our evolution. Such adversities have also left their mark on our intelligence and ability to communicate.

A useful discipline for understanding this process is evolutionary psychology, which is because the human brain and psychology developed over thousands of years in order to survive in particular conditions. These conditions have been variable and, in some cases, quite different from the current ones, leading to evolutionary advantages under conditions different from those of our modern world. That phenomenon is known as evolutionary disparity.[99]

---

99   "The Evolutionary Psychology of Politics." n.d.

The big question is, how did that complexity come about? How did primates become politicians? To find the answer, let's travel back in time to our roots as a species. How did it all begin? When did we begin to take on our own identity as modern humans?

There are records indicating that the first humans began to spread beyond the African continent more than 1.9 million years ago, migrating towards Asia in what would soon become a global conquest. Archaeological findings in Africa from over 400,000 years ago show a rapid rise in the number of stone tools, pointing to increasing technological capabilities. Together with this growing innovativeness evidenced by the manufacture of tools came greater degrees of complexity among human groups. Around this time, behaviors such as alliances and exchange of goods among groups begin to appear more markedly. This complexity expands with such speed that we know that 130,000 years ago the hominins (our ancestors) were able to trade materials over distances greater than 300 km, while evidence of the capacity to communicate through symbols dates from at least 250,000 years ago.[100]

The increase in the number of stone tools marks the consolidation of the Stone Age, which is divided

Psychology Today. https://www.psychologytoday.com/blog/darwins-subterranean-world/201510/the-evolutionary-psychology-politics.
100   Smithsonian's National Museum of Natural History. 2010. "Climate Effects on Human Evolution." The Smithsonian Institution's Human Origins Program. March 2010. http://humanorigins.si.edu/research/climate-and-human-evolution/climate-effects-human-evolution.

into the Paleolithic, Mesolithic and Neolithic periods. The Paleolithic played out mainly during the Ice Age (Pleistocene) between 2,600,000 and 11,700 years ago, but records exist of stone tools that are around 3.3 million years old. During the Paleolithic, men hunted wild animals, fish and birds, while women gathered fruits and nuts. The Paleolithic ended 11,700 years ago, giving way to the Mesolithic, which occurred during the Holocene (considered by many as an interglacial era) and lasted until 9,700 years ago. The Mesolithic saw extensive human movement along with major cultural changes that had been developing throughout the Pleistocene, probably due to the abundance of food following the end of the Ice Age. There is substantial evidence for good collective organization throughout the Mesolithic for activities such as hunting.

In the Paleolithic, Homo habilis and Homo erectus were the predominant human species. Both groups dispersed across Africa and Eurasia and were able to make tools such as picks and axes, even incorporating artistic motifs. It is thought that they lived in caves and tent-like shelters, gathering in groups known as bands, with a hierarchical structure that was probably limited to the immediate family.[101]

The oldest known fire pits date back 790,000 years and there are those who think that the cooking of food has been practiced for more than one-and-a-half

---

101   "A Description of Early Stone Age Cultures." n.d. The Classroom | Empowering Students in Their College Journey. http://classroom.synonym.com/description-ear-ly-stone-age-cultures-22052.html.

million years. Fire made it possible to extract nutrients by making food easier to digest and eliminating some plant poisons. Fires also served as a meeting place as people gathered in search of heat and to share food and socialize. The surge in the size and complexity of the brain caused the period of growth and development of human offspring to increase, which extended the environment of parental protection and expanded social connections.[102] These changes led to the construction of shelters.

Many archaeological finds related to the first humans were made during the period between the World Wars, which explains why there was so much emphasis on violence. Word quickly spread that the findings showed high levels of violence among early humans, including cannibalism. However, extensive evidence has also been found to support the idea that for the most part, the humans collaborated for the first two million years.[103]

Human evolution continues to be the subject of much controversy in terms of how the evolutionary tree branched out over time.[104] Sometimes the controversy

---

102   "Hearths & Shelters." 2010. The Smithsonian Institution's Human Origins Program. January 8, 2010. http://humanorigins.si.edu/evidence/behavior/hearths-shelters.
103   March 2006, Heather Whipps 16. n.d. "Peace or War? How Early Humans Behaved." Livescience.Com. http://www.livescience.com/640-peace-war-early-humans-behaved.html.
104   "The Emergence of Humans." n.d. Evolution.Berkeley.Edu. http://evolution.berkeley.edu/evolibrary/article/evograms_07.

centers around which species shared a common trunk with our ancestors (hominids), and which species were our direct ancestors (hominins).

Modern humans evolved over the past 600,000 years, and it has only been 200,000 years since our species first appeared in Africa and began migrating to Asia and Europe.[105]

The span between 200,000 and 50,000 years ago is known as the Middle Paleolithic. It is thought that some bands during this time were still nomadic, made up of 20 to 100 members. Apparently, there were already agreements between bands as well as the exchange of raw materials. In the Upper Paleolithic (between 50,000- and 10,000-years BCE) there were already signs of art, musical instruments, sculptures, and more advanced tools. It is thought that modern Homo sapiens appeared in this era, but archaeologists disagree as to whether formal leadership or division of labor based on hierarchies existed at this time.

According to DNA studies, the Neanderthals lived in small groups isolated from each other, which could have hindered natural selection through the elimination disadvantageous genes. Interestingly, the genes involved in hyperactivity and aggressive behavior in modern humans do not seem to have been present in Neanderthals.[106]

---

105   "Cro-Magnon Man." n.d. TheFreeDictionary.Com. http://encyclopedia2.thefreedictionary.com/Cro-Mag-non+man.
106   "Neanderthals Lived in Small, Isolated Populations, Gene Analysis Shows." 2014. National Geographic News. April 22, 2014. http://news.nationalgeographic.com/

The Cro-Magnons may have appeared around 45,000 years ago. Apparently, they still lived in caves and moved about only to hunt or in response to environmental changes. They had a great appreciation for art and buried their dead[107]. Finely finished stone and bone tools, as well as ivory jewelry and polychromatic paintings, show the level of cultural advancement of the Cro-Magnons, and has given rise to theory that the extinction of the Neanderthals was due to their inability to compete with the Cro-Magnons.

Recently, anthropologists have paid interest to the study of the first human societies which consisted of groups of hunters and gatherers, with a view to understanding human nature and the evolution of different cultures. Agriculture was not practiced until starting about 10,000 years ago, then went on to replace the original hunting and gathering societies over hundreds of years[108]. It is doubtful that human nature has evolved much since the introduction of agriculture, since evolution is a slow process in human terms, implying changes that take between 50,000 and 100,000 years, alternated with periods of stability.[109]

news/2014/04/140421-neanderthal-dna-genes-human-an-cestry-science/.

107   "Cro-Magnon | Prehistoric Human." n.d. Encyclopedia Britannica. https://www.britannica.com/topic/Cro-Magnon.

108   Ember, Carol R. 2014. "Hunter-Gatherers (Foragers)." *Hraf.Yale.Edu*, July. http://hraf.yale.edu/ehc/summaries/hunter-gatherers.

109   2015. Amazonaws.Com. 2015. https://s3.amazonaws.com/ww-article-cache-1/es/Introducci%25C3%25B-3n_a_la_evoluci%25C3%25B3n.

The first humans were organized into small groups of approximately 30 individuals from different families, depending on the availability of food in a given place, and subsisted as nomads dedicated to hunting and gathering. They followed the movement of the animals they hunted, sharing knowledge, tools and gene pools along the way. At the same time, they also engaged in violent conflicts that caused them to fear each other.[110]

These hunter-gatherer societies required extensive areas to supply their needs, estimated at anywhere between 18 and 1,300 square km of land per person, and had to go wherever food sources were. Such a culture allowed for only small groupings of humans, since a large group could quickly deplete food sources. The groups that moved on foot may have had around 30 individuals, while it is believed that groups that moved with animals such as horses could reach around 100 individuals.[111]

Bonds of affinity and camaraderie were essential in hunter-gatherer societies and probably served to define societal roles along with age and sex. The political institutions would have been very rudimentary. Control may have been exercised through revenge, group pressure, and fear of the supernatural. There was practically a kind of primitive communism in these

110   "Chapter 2: The Earliest Human Societies Lesson 1 Hunters and Gatherers MAIN IDEAS." n.d. http://www.eduplace.com/ss/socsci/ca/books/bkf3/reviews/pdfs/LS_6_02_01.pdf.
111   "Hunter-Gatherer | Definition, Societies, & Facts." n.d. Encyclopedia Britannica. https://www.britannica.com/topic/hunting-and-gathering-culture.

societies as inequities were minimal and the concept of private property was limited to the things that the individual constantly used.[112]

Present-day hunter-gatherer cultures continue to share some of the same characteristics: they are small, semi-nomadic, have no political leader, and remain egalitarian. They do not teach children to obey, show more affection to children, talk less among themselves and are less vulnerable to crises due to unpredictable events such as food shortages. Compared to cultures that produce their own food, hunter-gatherers fight less. Societies that are more dependent on collection tend to be more matriarchal, while those that are more dependent on hunting tend to be more patriarchal.

The Mesolithic period, considered by some to be the last stage of the Paleolithic, occurred between 20,000 and 10,000 years ago, followed by the Neolithic. Agriculture appeared with the beginning of the Neolithic around 12,000 years ago and brought profound transformations to human societies, which is why this period has been called "the Neolithic revolution." With agriculture and a relatively stable food supply, the egalitarian hunter-gatherer groups formed settlements[113]. Agriculture also brought a dramatic increase in the human population, which concentrated in communities and in greater numbers. This can be considered the beginning of what

---

112   *2017. [online] Available at: <http://www2.fiu. edu/~grenierg/chapter5.htm> [Accessed 17 November 2017].*
113   "The Development of Agriculture." 2019. Geno-graphic Project. 2019. https://genographic.nationalgeo-graphic.com/development-of-agriculture/.

would become the first civilizations, which would lead to the search for knowledge and mastery. Population growth, specialization of labor, and the rapid increase in collective knowledge gave rise to laws and hierarchies. The need to save and pass on knowledge probably stimulated the development of writing as the best tool for storing information and handing it down from generation to generation[114]. The first records of writing correspond to cuneiform texts dating from only 3,000 to 3,500 years before Christ and were developed by the Sumerians in Mesopotamia (what is now Iraq).[115]

The origin of agriculture, however, was not unique to one area. Agriculture appeared at different times and in different places between 10,000 and 15,000 years ago. Humans were introducing changes in the environment which led to changes in the species of plants and animals as they were being domesticated. Apparently, the first animal to be domesticated was the dog, with only three mothers giving rise to 95% of the dog breeds that accompany us today. The development of agriculture increased the supply of food, medicines, fibers, and other resources.[116]

The cultural adaptations prompted by the end of the Pleistocene, together with the development of food production, allowed for a greater degree of development

114   Khan Academy. 2019. "7. Agriculture & Civilization." Khan Academy. 2019. https://www.khanacademy.org/part-ner-content/big-history-project/agriculture-civilization.
115   "Cuneiform." n.d. Ancient History Encyclopedia. http://www.ancient.eu/cuneiform/.
116   "Origins of Agriculture." 2019. In *Encyclopædia Britannica*. https://www.britannica.com/topic/agriculture.

in human cultures. The Neolithic period, on the other hand, coincided with climatic shifts that triggered important changes in flora and fauna.[117]

Throughout the Neolithic (approximately 10,000 to 3,000 years before Christ), together with the emergence of agriculture, the domestication of animals and the development of trade, the first advances in architecture and engineering were also taking place.

Unlike the Paleolithic hunter-gatherers, nomadic groups following the Neolithic revolution have retained certain characteristics of the settled communities with which they maintain contact. Modern nomadic cultures have adopted the institutions of post-Neolithic societies, along with their social structures and moral concepts. The interaction between nomads and societies of settled communities has led to their mutual influence on each other throughout history.[118]

The Bronze Age begins with the end of the Neolithic and extends from 3,000 to 1,000 years before Christ; it is followed by the Iron Age, which begins 1,000 years before Christ and extends to the present. The Bronze Age is defined by the ability to extract and melt metal to forge or mold it. Humans started using iron when they reached a level of technology that allowed them to bring metals to the high temperatures necessary to melt them. The big difference in

117   "Stone Age | Definition, Tools, Art, & Facts." n.d. Encyclopedia Britannica. https://www.britannica.com/event/Stone-Age.
118   "Nomadic and Settled Peoples in Steppe Land-scapes and within Statehood: SFB 586 · Differenz Und Inte-gration." n.d. Www.Nomadsed.De. http://www.nomadsed.de/en/nomaden-sesshafte/introduction/.

being able to use iron is that it is much more abundant than copper, allowing for the large-scale production of different types of tools and weapons[119]. However, the advance in prehistoric societies was asymmetric; different civilizations reached the Bronze Age and the Iron Age at different times (like what was observed in the introduction of agriculture). Thus, for example, in pre-Columbian America only the Incas reached the Bronze Age, while Europeans came to master the forging of iron and other metals.

From writing to agriculture to the use of bronze to the manufacture of iron weapons, we could continue our journey through human history until we reach modern society, marked by the Industrial Revolution that began in the 18th century. It was during this time that use of steam engines spread. A Second Industrial Revolution, characterized using electricity and assembly lines, followed. Then came the Third Industrial Revolution, introducing the widespread use of computers. It is thought that the Fourth Industrial Revolution will consist of the combination of real and virtual systems, with great advances in physical, digital and biological technology that are expected to have major impacts on economy and industry.[120] However, it is best that we

---

119   "Stone, Bronze, and Iron Ages | Essential Human-ities." 2013. Essential-Humanities.Net. 2013. http://www. essential-humanities.net/history-overview/stone-bronze-iron-ages/.

120   Marr, Bernard. n.d. "Why Everyone Must Get Ready For The 4th Industrial Revolution." Forbes. https://www.forbes.com/sites/bernardmarr/2016/04/05/why-everyone-must-get-ready-for-4th-industrial-revolu-tion/#70a416493f90.

delve no further into historical technicalities and return to our issue of power relations. One of the oldest causes of asymmetry in power has been religion, but...how did it come about?

Origin of religions

This is a great question. How is it that some humans are willing to commit suicide bombings, wage fierce wars, or simply give up ten percent of the product of their work in the name of religion? What has led us to this? How did a group of primates come to believe themselves superior to the rest of nature, and to have the arrogance to regard themselves as the image and likeness of the creative force of the entire universe?

The answer is simpler than one might think. It has nothing to do with aliens or deities. It only takes a bit of reconciliation between faith, reason and objectivity. We know that our senses do not allow us to perceive everything that exists and that science is only able to study what our technology allows us to measure, but for a moment, let's travel back to the beginning (... *our* beginning ...).

It all starts with something as simple as death. Of course, death and what comes after it are anything but a simple matter, but it is not worth theorizing about a subject which I do not understand, which you probably do not understand either, and which no one will likely ever understand. Remember, this is a book about power relations and evolution. For a moment, let's reduce the problem to the fact that there is evidence that the Neanderthals were the first hominids to bury their dead. While there are those who argue that the first indications of religion appeared 300,000 years ago, little evidence exists to support such statements, making this position controversial. The first indication of religion was the burial of the dead; however, there is also possible evidence of adoration of animal deities and the use of symbology.

More abundant evidence for funeral ceremonies began to appear around 50,000 years ago. At that time, our ancestors placed animal bones, tools, and even flowers next to the body of the deceased. These findings make it clear that death consciousness and its implications were already present. There are those who think that the burial of the dead began to avoid the inconvenience caused by the decomposition of corpses or simply to prevent the arrival of scavengers. These latter views support the controversy over the existence of religious beliefs among the Neanderthals.[121]

The Cro-Magnon paintings found in caves suggest religious symbolism and funeral ceremonies. Religion appears to have its beginnings in the belief in life after death and the first religions were animistic, that is, they believed that everything had a spirit of its own (including hunted animals). It is thought that prayers were offered for a variety of reasons, such as getting rid of vermin.[122]

---

121   "Religion - When, Why and How Did It Begin?" n.d. Www.Garvandwane.Com. http://www.garvandwane.com/religion/early_religion.html.

122   "Studying Societies at JHK / Early Human Cave Paintings and Religion." n.d. Studyingsocietiesatjhk.Pb-works.Com. http://studyingsocietiesatjhk.pbworks.com/w/page/18798571/Early%20Human%20Cave%20Paintings%20and%20Religion

Now, the big question is, at what point in time did the problem of death give way to belief in supernatural forces? We know that during the Upper Paleolithic figurines in human form began to appear, suggesting the belief in supernatural beings. This occurred approximately 30,000 years ago.[123]

It is not hard to imagine how verbal traditions would have led to exaggerations about the achievements or virtues of the dead ancestors of a human group (remember that all this occurs before the development of writing). These exaggerations, product of the passing of the verbal tradition, could have played a key role in leading humans to perceive their dead relatives as deities (in fact, multiple ancient religions mixed divine characteristics with human characteristics, or incorporated the figure of the "demigod"). The more time that passed following the death of admired individuals, and the more generations that passed, the greater the attributes, virtues, and achievements assigned to them (it would be expected that the first religions were polytheistic). Similarly, it would be expected that the more generations that passed following a given event, the greater the distortion in the narrative from one generation to the next.

Superstition, we can say, has united human cultures across the planet; it is also easily transmitted within families. Believing in "something" supernatural seems to make situations that go beyond our ability to control less stressful. This suggestion confers an evolutionary

---

123   *Fallio V. New Developments in Consciousness Re-search. Nova Science Publishers, Inc. New York. 2007.*

advantage to our superstitious mind since the existence of "something" supernatural offers us the possibility of asking for help. The possibility of having someone to ask for help through some ritual reduces stress (even though the inevitable happens anyway). Superstition also brings unity to society; if there is something that transcends the mundane, it cannot be the property of an individual.[124]

Ancient religions are also thought to have been related to the harvest (particularly after the emergence of agriculture), which makes sense, since we cannot control the weather or pests, and both endanger the survival of an agricultural society. The feeling of having control over the factors that determine crop success may have been key to the institutionalization of religion within human societies.

Then, following agriculture, writing appeared, changing the way traditions were passed down through the generations. Nevertheless, the distortions continued to multiply due to the evolution of language, cultural changes, changes in the environment, and often, due to ignorance of the context in which the original events took place.

Keeping in mind that this book is about power relationships, certain questions may arise: At what point did the problem of death begin to exercise control over social behaviors in the form of today's religions? How did a possible belief in life after death lead to the

---

124   2017. [online] Available at: <http://content.time.com/time/arts/article/0,8599,1890165,00.html> [Accessed 3 December 2017].

creation of organizations for social control among the many cultures of our world?

While the first religions of the Paleolithic period seem to have been egalitarian, in later religions shamans and religious authorities began to appear, occupying a dominant and privileged position within the social group. Social control seems to have consolidated when certain members of a group began claiming the ability to communicate with deceased ancestors (often perceived as deities).

Apparently, the ability to become the "means of communication" with the dead (or deities) made it possible to build social structures around an individual or a group of individuals. In that way, religions have been able to congregate large numbers of humans under a structure, often vertical. These structures are usually led by individuals who could be the equivalent of alpha males, but the adherents do not reject the hierarchical order and join voluntarily. Such behavior can be interpreted as typical of primate groups that perceive the presence of an external threat. However, the exact nature of this external threat varies; it could be a fear of death, sin, hell, or simply, the natural fear of the unknown.

As one might expect, the concentration of human power has been accompanied by a similar concentration of power among the deities, leading to monotheism (as the Spanish saying goes: The thief judges by his condition. We humans project our own nature on others.)

Human nature

In the middle ages, Ibn Khaldun observed in his work *Muqaddimah* that we humans need to live in societies because it is easier for us to obtain food and defend ourselves from predators. Simple game theory reinforces this idea; we know that in small groups, we are more likely to achieve some sort of coordination. The degree of coordination will depend on the similarity in the benefits received by the different members of the group.

The evolutionary basis of primate societies is cooperation in small groups. However, the size reached by human societies, our selfish interests, and individual conflicts make the concept of morals indispensable. Morality allows us to resolve our internal conflicts within the social environment without affecting the rest of the group. Primatologist Frans De Waal states that "religion is not irrelevant, but it is not the basis of morality".[125]

Here is an example of evolutionary disparity: since we originally lived in small nomadic groups, our cerebral neocortex is only able to store information on about 150 people. It is not adapted for dealing with large groups such as those that began to form with the advent of agriculture, much less for understanding complex "international" situations.

---

125   Video, Teen Young. 2014. "'La Moral Humana Viene de Los Simios' Ciencia y Religión." Taringa! June 21, 2014. http://www.taringa.net/post/ciencia-educacion/17911931/La-moral-humana-viene-de-los-simios-Ciencia-y-Religion.html.

We already know that humans constantly seek access to more and better resources, which is reflected in social position. Resources are obtained through selfishness, asymmetric mutualism and reciprocal altruism; the latter even applies to the concept of corruption (understanding corruption as the abuse of a public power for personal gain). Reciprocal altruism and asymmetric mutualism develop in conjunction with the ability to negotiate and are more socially acceptable than selfishness as a way of acquiring power or access to resources. Both asymmetric mutualism and asymmetric altruism imply mutual gain but with greater benefits to one of the parties, who will be socially strengthened or enriched following the exchange of favors.

As with other primate groups, among humans, favors are paid with favors. And while it is true that charity makes people happier and healthier,[126] it is also true that, as in all animal societies, climbing the hierarchical ladder can be achieved through negotiation and exchange of favors.

In fact, there are those who argue that Neanderthals practiced altruism only within small groups, which leaves the question of whether the lack of "universal" altruism was partly the cause of their extinction.

Reciprocal altruism is also practiced between countries; such exchanges strengthen the country that is best equipped to negotiate to obtain the greatest benefit.

In human societies, enrichment, understood as access to more resources of the best quality, occurs

126   "Why Generous People End Up Getting The Most Out Of Life." n.d. Elite Daily. http://elitedaily.com/life/generous-people-end-getting-life/1102628/.

because of asymmetric mutualistic relationships and even as a product of selfish relationships, mainly in systems where control institutions do not function well. Of course, selfishness is never well viewed, but one cannot doubt its effectiveness in certain cases.

As time passed, growing intelligence and the beginning of civilization made competition for resources more complex among humans. It also introduced competition factors not present among other primates, such as structured knowledge.

Knowledge took on a particularly important role in social complexity with the invention of the printing press. Printing was an important accomplishment (perhaps the most important in humanity, after writing) which contributed in an unprecedented way to the expansion and dissemination of knowledge. Initially, it contributed to the expansion of European imperialism; subsequently, it led to social empowerment and the sparking of revolutions. Curiously, with this empowerment of the masses a new level of social complexity is introduced, leading to the formation of authoritarian governments (example: Napoleon) as the only apparent way of maintaining social order. Once order has been re-established at this new level of social complexity, a more equitable and participatory political system is established.

Another source of conflict inherent to humans is envy (remember the Capuchin monkeys). Envy is nothing more than the natural rejection of the idea that someone has access to more resources or wields greater power, giving them the possibility of harming others with impunity. Envy is the driver of every resentful group wishing to challenge the existing social structure or replace the elite but lacking the means to achieve it. This can create problems at any social level, from governments to corporations, or simply within the family nucleus. There will always be individuals who – whether by choice or condition - do nothing, but who also do not allow others to do anything, so that no one stand outs or excels or is able to claim subsequent benefits.

The previous observations help us better understand why corruption bothers us so much. Here's how it works: corrupt individuals use resources that do not belong to them to establish a mutualistic relationship, offering collective property in exchange for personal benefits. This is interpreted by the group as: 1) damage to the rest of the group, by offering their goods without their consent; 2) asymmetric access to the best resources, given that the corrupt person has a greater ability to monopolize resources with less effort, when compared to the rest of society. All this places him (or her) in a position of power over the rest, which is seen as a threat to equity in the social system and arouses feelings of envy. It is no wonder that social clamor demands the expulsion, imprisonment or even death of those who resort to such practices.

Competition for resources, together with the natural behaviors of our species and the social complexity resulting from our intelligence, have caused human civilizations to require an authority that prevents its members from attacking each other. The creation of institutions that neutralize violence is an evolutionary advantage, since it allows for a growing population while promoting cooperative behaviors and reducing the social cost that conflicts entail.

Human societies have become true living organisms. Just as cells are grouped to form multicellular beings, so multicellular organisms can be grouped together to form social systems, respecting natural biological tendencies. Our societies, like all other living beings, are born, grow, reproduce, and die. This is well known by those who study organizational systems, but here we are trying to understand it from the evolutionary point of view. The desire to reproduce and avoid death has given rise to expansionist cultures including all the empires of antiquity, as well as communism, the concept of the Western "free world", and, without a doubt, Islamic extremism. In the end, all the above are manifestations of societies that behave like living beings and compete with other similar living beings, either through reproduction, survival, or simple hoarding of resources.

Mathematics demonstrates that human civilization behaves like a living organism, with collective behavior adding up to more than the sum of individual behaviors. This can be observed, for example, in military and business organizations, and is due to an increasing coordination among its members, where the specialization and diversity of individuals allow for greater influence on the environment. In biological systems, the most basic way to increase the impact of a coordinated collective behavior is through the control exercised by an individual over the movement of the rest of the group.[127]

---

127   "Complexity Rising: From Human Beings to Human Civilization, a Complexity Profile." n.d. New England Complex Systems Institute. http://necsi.edu/projects/yaneer/ Civilization.html.

Groups of countries are also known to expel or punish those who appear to pose a danger to others. It is not surprising that anti-imperialist cliques form (remember the envy) when there is a country that seems to concentrate enough power to harm others with impunity, or that possesses a disproportionately greater ability to access resources in greater quantities and/or quality.

It seems that human groups follow patterns that do not escape the natural tendency, no matter how superior we may think we are. The question is, could it be that what will happen in terms of the organization of humanity is predictable? Moreover, has it always been possible to predict everything that has happened throughout our history?

Well, experts in biomimicry say that the geometry of nature frequently incorporates spheres and spirals. Is it possible that spherical, circular and spiral patterns have been present all along in our organization and history, but our inability to recognize groups larger than 150 individuals has prevented us from seeing ourselves as a whole? How can a primate society resemble a spiral or a sphere? Is there a social "core"? Perhaps so. If humans congregate around resources, it is to be expected that there will be a group with greater evolutionary advantages (or simply, circumstantial advantages) that place them closer to the resources, forming a nucleus around them. If we see each other from the outside, we can identify a kind of social "crust" (to give it a name) which is in greater contact with the natural environment and that serves as protection for the "core" of society, although it is less close to the resources that hold the core together. Between the nuclear group and the crust there is always an intermediate layer that is closer to the resources than the crust, but also closer to the natural environment than the core. This could be the reason for social classes and hierarchies. If we view this trend from a global perspective, it is not surprising that the dependency theory has emerged, classifying nations into central, satellite and peripheral. It is no different from what we observed previously, only on a larger scale.

Finally, if we are going to talk about human nature, we cannot omit the most inhuman aspect of humans: our collective emotions. A collective behavior refers to group actions taken in a disorganized manner, in which the norms, laws and/or values of a society are challenged. There are three types of emotions expressed by human multitudes: panic, euphoria and anger.

Collective panic has probably been with us since the Pleistocene, when our psychobiological reactions to fear must have been extremely useful for preserving life.[128] Or perhaps it is only part of the nature of all animal societies (the disorganization caused by collective panic can be seen when we disturb a row of ants or a beehive).

Now comes the big question: What are the things that trigger panic, and why? We know that stress must first reach a critical level; after that, any additional stress will tip the balance, unleashing a panic attack.

---

128   Mooney, Chris. n.d. "Scientists Are Beginning to Figure out Why Conservatives Are...conservative." Mother Jones. http://www.motherjones.com/politics/2014/07/biology-ideology-john-hibbing-negativity-bias.

That stress may be caused by an alarm related to a life-threatening event (for example). We also know that the panic threshold (the size of the proverbial camel's back) seems to vary according to inherited/familial components[129] and, undoubtedly, to previous experience.

The other thing we might ask is, why is panic collective, if the stress threshold of each individual is different? That is a difficult question to answer. There are scientists who describe a collective consciousness, in which animals share connected behaviors ...uh... telepathically? Pretty far out there, right? Well, there is at least one report of some monkeys in Japan adopting identical behaviors without ever having contact with each other[130]. Likewise, we know that there are things that we will never fully understand, and that go beyond the scope of this book. So, let's turn now to:

Power games

If you have lived your entire life under the fantasy that human power games have their roots in grand business ideas, imperialism, or the last war to bring humanity to its knees, I am sorry to inform you that you are wrong. Power games start with speech! Yes, you heard me: the

---

129   Arkowitz, Hal, and Scott O. Lilienfeld. 2008. "Why Do We Panic?" *Scientific American Mind* 19 (5): 78–79. https://doi.org/10.1038/scientificamericanmind1008-78.
130   Woollaston, Victoria. 2013. "Are We PSYCHIC? Scientists Claim Humans Have Collective Consciousness." Mail Online. November 19, 2013. http://www.dailymail.co.uk/sciencetech/article-2509971/Are-PSYCHIC-Scientists-believe-animals--including-humans--collective-consciousness.html.

complexity of our brains, our societies, and our human interactions require excellent communication, and it is precisely there where power begins to develop within a group. There is evidence that the individuals who speak the most in a human group more easily take the lead, regardless of the value of what they say, what they know, what they do, or even their reason for wanting to take the lead. Other aspects that promote a person to leadership are the confidence with which they express themself and the authority they project. Men seem to project more self-confidence and authority than women, which explains why social leadership positions continue to be filled by men for the most part. And don't forget the ants: knowledge is a factor that influences the rise of a leader, since it is understood that it can get the group to where there are more resources.[131]

In humans, leadership mainly emerges when there is a large information gap between the members of a group and their leader. As expected, knowledge will often be connected in some way to age, and this is precisely what has traditionally, in many cultures, given the position of greatest hierarchy to the oldest individual. With a large group, a small informed group is enough to lead them. When there are conflicts of interest, experiments show that the majority interest usually prevails. When the group of informed leaders is small, a single additional informed leader can make a decisive

131   King, Andrew J., Dominic D.P. Johnson, and Mark Van Vugt. 2009. "The Origins and Evolution of Leadership." Current Biology 19 (19): R911–16. https://doi.org/10.1016/j.cub.2009.07.027.

difference. In humans, there are abundant tactics to guide a group. These are used by clergy, politicians, military officers, administrators, etc. The level of distribution of leadership can affect the contribution and cooperation of individuals. Collective action can be affected by non-cooperating individuals who also benefit from the group. The solution in these cases seems to be punishment or the threat of punishment, as a less expensive act. The attenuated dominance in the first egalitarian human groups facilitated the transition to democracy and the coordination of groups. Language, without a doubt, played an important role in this process.

The complexity in human civilization is the product of structural changes and the actual dynamics. In our time, there are more and more complex connections, with growing interdependence among the social system, economy, hierarchies in corporations, and political systems. Control within that interconnection can be understood as the influence that an individual exerts on the behavior of others. Coordination in human systems refers to the fact that individuals, despite doing different things, maintain a relationship among their activities. And while hierarchy helps maintain small-scale coordination, it also limits the level of complexity that can be achieved. Since there is a controller, the level of complexity of the operation is capped by the capacity of the controller.

In human societies there is also lateral control, which refers to the network connection between sub-systems of a society. Apparently, the tendency in humans is to seek a greater distribution of control, which leads to a network of influences (remember the first egalitarian hunter-gatherer communities). All this has forced hierarchies to evolve on par with social complexity, which has had an impact on the ramifications and lateral interactions. Progress towards larger systems throughout human history has gone hand in hand with the centralization of power. The increasing complexity in the tasks has caused the complexity of the entire system to increase as the system branches out into other, smaller layers. The hierarchy would appear to succumb to the increasing complexity of collective behavior; at the same time, it seems to function as scaffolding that enables advancement to a new level of complexity.

Humans seem to have a deeply rooted instinct to exert power over others, while also feeling aversion for those who abuse power and a natural inclination to punish such abusers. However, the tendency to maintain equity in human groups has been observed since the first hunter-gatherer societies, which arrived at social contracts that sidelined personal ambitions of dominance. The equity practiced by these prehistoric societies is the principle that has led us to our modern democracies. In villages, even illiterate ones, there seems to be a predisposition towards equity, evidenced by the fact that male members who demonstrate selfish tendencies are often treated poorly as being morally deviant.

It is not surprising, then, that our social evolution has been caught between the lust for power and the desire for social equity, making power a problem of our species. In some instances, the concentration of power has enabled certain countries to function, while in others, autocratic governments backed by military forces have generated mixed support. Society certainly understands the benefits of a powerful governing figure, especially when the group becomes large, very complex, and, quite simply, very difficult to manage. In this context, the alpha male fulfills the function of maintaining internal order while minimizing the damage caused by internal struggles. Such a figure can even be viewed positively if he also shows generosity.

The tendency to dominate seems to be intrinsic, a heritage of our common ancestor. Therefore, if equality is to be maintained in a human society, there must be consequences - isolation, public exposure or definitive expulsion - to contain our innate thirst for power. It can be assumed that natural leaders will want to increase their power, which is why we have laws to restrict their power and guarantee the rights of citizens. Furthermore, an equitable distribution of power seems to be necessary to maintain social peace. Societies that do not keep an eye on their leaders tend to assume hierarchical forms like those of other major primates. It is for this reason that egalitarian democracies must carefully monitor the rise of dictatorships, to limit their power. The ambivalent nature of humanity seems to be extrapolated to the community of nations, in which a superpower can maintain order but can also take the form of a tyrant, with disastrous consequences.[132]

The above can be quite confusing. There is an ambivalence towards authority in our societies. On the one hand, taxation is required to maintain order, and

---

132   "Political Primates." n.d. Greater Good. http://greatergood.berkeley.edu/article/item/political_primates.

on the other hand, equity is required to limit abuses by particular individuals. This dilemma has been resolved by modern democracies through institutions which try to ensure that everyone respects the law equally. But why hasn't it always been like this? More importantly, will it ever stop being like this? The answer seems to be: it depends. There are circumstances that require authoritarian hierarchical systems to bring a society through certain situations without succumbing to chaos. The implementation of rapid changes may require a dominant, hard-handed leader so that order can be maintained. Then there are moments of relative stability in which the horizontal hierarchical order is restored. In other words: crises bring opportunities which open the door for society to demand order, and order paves the way for equity.

Let's put it this way: Humanity has been constantly evolving in a virtuous cycle, in which our intelligence is reinforced by social complexity. Each time the complexity of our society has historically increased, authoritarian regimes have taken over. But each time there are periods of relative stability, the masses demand the establishment of a more horizontal authority.

To better understand what I will call the "Evolutionary theory of politics," let's analyze the shift from reigns to republics. The growth of human groups required order to maintain unity in the face of increasing complexity, compelling these groups to support the authority of an "alpha male", even one with traits of tyranny. Once order was established, the egalitarian tendencies observed in the first human societies resurfaced, causing political structures to evolve into republics or simply to more participatory and horizontal systems. The behavior observed among different cultures seems to be one of seeking order first to avoid the damage caused by internal conflicts, followed by a search for equity.

Based on this "evolutionary theory of politics," we can see that the success of vertical systems depends on how equitable the distribution of access to resources is, while the success of equitable horizontal systems will depend on the ability of their institutions to ensure order. To put it another way, the weakness of authoritarianism lies in the unequal distribution of power, while the main weakness of democracy is the lack of authority.

In short, we cannot rule out the presence of violence on humanity's fluctuating path between order and equity, between authoritarianism and social participation. It seems that violence and conflicts depend on the balance of power in a society, while changes in the balance of power often depend on violence. Revolutions in the quest for equity, as they expand (in terms of population and geographic extension), begin to challenge more and more aspects of the previous order, necessitating even more violence to establish a new authority (who imposes order once again, followed by a new, more extensive system of equity). This is clearly stated by Henry Kissinger in his book *World Order*, where he says that reigns of terror are not an accident, but inherent to revolutions.

Usually in a relationship of asymmetric power, peace prevails until one party believes it can defeat the other. In this way, war occurs when the two sides feel that there is a close balance of power between them.

It is for this reason that civil society must negotiate objectives, and only challenge power when it has sufficient resources to change the balance of power within society.

In addition to dealing with increasing social complexity, the tendency to congregate under a hierarchical vertical structure seems to be effective in the face of an external threat. This has been well known and exploited by authoritarian governments to maintain internal order in a country. If an external threat is perceived, the choice of the strongest member as leader would be aimed at guaranteeing the survival of the group. A fundamental characteristic of authoritarianism is the tendency to lump together external and internal threats in a rhetoric that appeals to popular emotions and beliefs,[133] as has been observed innumerable times throughout history.

Modern life

Something that has radically changed power relations within modern society is the concept of private property, which requires the capacity for and development of abstract thinking. James Kriert, in his essay "Evolutionary Theory and the Origin of Property Rights", points out that the concept of private property appeared unintentionally, with objects of personal use. As we can imagine, for a band of hunter-gatherers, the abstract concept of land ownership would not fit

133   "From Post-Truth to Post-Lies." n.d. Psychology Today. https://www.psychologytoday.com/blog/intention-al-insights/201703/post-truth-post-lies.

with their way of life, although they did understand the concept of territory. Undoubtedly, the trigger for the concept of land ownership may have been the introduction of agriculture. Of course, agriculture facilitated the idea of property through repeated use of the land, just as the concept of property stimulated the interest of the individual in growing crops and investing in improving the land. However, in his book *From Jungles to Paddocks,* Stanley Heckadon shows us that even at the beginning of the 20th century there was no concept of land ownership among Hispanic peasants in the Isthmus of Panama, even though they already had a very well established subsistence agriculture. A clash between agriculture and the concept of scarcity was necessary before land acquired a "considerable value", paving the way for the concept of land ownership.

With the right to property, social asymmetries begin to appear, as can be observed in almost every culture in the world (there will always be those who blame social asymmetries on imperialism and capitalism). But didn't the Egyptians and Romans have slaves? Apparently, the right to property instilled the confidence to increase both production and trade, which have been the drivers of the economy over centuries of growth but have also generated some of the inequities present in our modern Western societies. The right to property has led to the creation of new institutions to maintain social order, since the different forms of property have steadily increased in value, making them worth "fighting" for.

It is no secret that free supply and demand have been the basis of so much of our technological advancement in recent centuries. But it is a principle that requires equity for there to be genuine competition in work and creativity. That equity depends on regulatory institutions to maintain order, but let us not forget that we are talking about maintaining control over members of an increasingly intelligent and sophisticated species (remember the Capuchin monkeys who used coins and ended up practicing robbery, fraud and prostitution). It would seem that inherent to the concept of free supply and demand is a constant competition not only between consumers and suppliers, but also among institutions and groups of individuals who, by nature, try to evade the norms (not to mention organized crime).

Another gear inserted into our social machinery has been the advance in telecommunications, which we will discuss later in this book.

In short, while free trade requires that society expand to generate more wealth, that expansion also makes society more complex and difficult to control.

In that vein, it is interesting to note that elitism appears to be intrinsic to our nature. There is no way to organize a group of animals without adequate communication, or without the coordination of an individual or small group of individuals. It seems that the structuring of an elite class is inseparable from the asymmetry in information. At the same time, our inherent search for equality can lead us to challenge the dominant elite, especially during times when the need for a leader is not perceived. That is literally the function of revolutions: to replace existing elites.

Our social characteristics seem to adhere to the order of priority established by evolution throughout our development as a species. Equality is the ultimate desirable characteristic in human societies.

That same social equality seems to be the tendency among nations, while at times clashing with the instinct to strive for leadership. As Henry Kissinger rightly mentions in his book *Diplomacy*, societies with an equitable balance of power are difficult to achieve among nations. Among the few examples are the city-states of ancient Greece and the European system created by the Peace of Westphalia in 1648.

The point is: Could it be that those ancient Greek city-states knew more than we do about the role of distribution in the balance of power? Has politics always been intrinsic to our species, as it is now, in modern times? Or is it simply that no exact definition of politics exists? Let's continue to the next chapter...

VII. Politics within a society

Once we have seen that power relations are intrinsic to nature itself and found in virtually all ecosystems, and that interactions occur at all levels in nature, we can have a little better understanding of the origin of politics and its role in human societies.

As mentioned in the previous chapter, the concept developed by the great philosopher Aristotle, who related politics to the communal welfare of citizens,[134] is questionable. The word *politics* comes from the Greek *politikos,* which in turn is rooted in the word *polis*, meaning *city*, and has been used since the sixteenth century with different meanings. The concept of politics can have multiple definitions, ranging from the art and science of guiding or influencing government actions, to competition between interest groups for power and control of government.[135]

---

134   "Aristotle: Politics | Internet Encyclopedia of Philosophy." n.d. Www.Iep.Utm.Edu. http://www.iep.utm.edu/aris-pol/.
135   "Definition of POLITICS." 2019. Merriam-Webster.Com. 2019. https://www.merriam-webster.com/dictionary/politics.

Power can be defined as the ability to influence a group, but to frame it in somewhat clearer (and blunter) terms, we will refer to politics in the sense of access to resources, as explained in previous chapters. We can talk about the struggle for power, where "power" is understood to be the ability to get "what *you* have, which is valuable to *me*." If this definition sounds too harsh, we need only remember the war in Syria, the Iraqi oil fields, or the Crimean Peninsula. Another equally rudimentary way of understanding the concept is to define power as control over goods and services, in which one human being can acquire control of another through a process that can be understood as similar to a purchase.[136]

Politics is intrinsic to every human society at all levels. Power relations begin in the family, between siblings, parents and children, children and pets, etc. Politics is even practiced by the family dog when it learns to do whatever it takes to achieve a simple objective such as getting a bone, a walk or some table scraps from the humans that live in the same house. Power relations are found in schools, within companies, between companies, and of course, among groups interested in the political control of a country, as well as among countries interested in controlling access to valuable resources in order to establish a global order at their convenience.

Politics, as we now understand it, is part of every society of living beings regardless of their degree of

136   Baldwin, David A. 2010. "Money and Power*."
http://www.princeton.edu/~dbaldwin/selected%20articles/
Baldwin%20(1971)%20Money%20and%20Power.pdf.

evolution. It is part of the dynamics of interactions both within a social group and between different groups. Since power relations are found everywhere, their comparison using quantitative methods is easy. Such comparisons promise to provide a wealth of information about how living beings come together, cooperate and compete for life.

While it is common for power struggles to be associated with males, they also occur frequently in the female sex. Primatology studies originally focused exclusively on competition between males, discounting females as passive members of societies. However, Schiebinger argues that ignoring competition between females can cause a biased interpretation, by relegating the interaction between the sexes to a strictly reproductive sphere. Later studies have found that females play an active role in power games within society, and even lead groups. Strum described in his studies that the investment by males in maintaining good relations with females facilitated their rise in the hierarchy of social power. Schiebinger went on to show that female primates are also territorial and manage to form alliances and hierarchies of power in conjunction with males.

Originally, power relations in all species were defined by the struggle to find food and mates. However, advances in human technology have brought greater levels of complexity to basic needs, with the appearance of intermediate resources such as money, housing, access to health and education to achieve the natural biological goals of survival and reproduction.

Political science regards power relations much the same way economists regard money relations: money can be used to buy power, but it is not indispensable nor sufficient to guarantee the obtaining and control of power.

While it is true that we humans have a deep sense of competition for resources and are capable - like all primates - of reaching extreme levels of violence amongst ourselves and against other species, it is also true that the success of humans as a species has been achieved through cooperation. Despite natural competition, our species, as with others, also depends for its survival on positive interactions among its individuals. Cooperation among humans has allowed the mastery of many aspects of the environment and the rapid expansion of our population, which continues despite the inequities in our current world. Cooperation and trust are the amalgam that holds our societies together, and the loss of trust, with the subsequent loss of cooperation, can lead to an unstable power structure and social collapse. [137]We know that the greater the parallels between the interests within a group, the more cohesive it will be. That parallelism of interests is the key that defines any type of alliance.

All these interactions between forces led to the formal study of the distribution of power in the United States beginning in the 1950s, with each study arguing a distribution of power based on different measures of dominance.[138]

---

137   "Bloomberg - Are You a Robot?" n.d. Www. Bloomberg.Com. https://www.bloomberg.com/view/articles/2016-11-12/blame-rich-overeducated-elites-as-society-frays.
138   "Who Rules America: The Class-Domination Theory of Power." n.d. Whorulesamerica.Ucsc.Edu. http://www2.ucsc.edu/whorulesamerica/power/class_domination.html.

The interplay between cooperation and competition is key to the stability of all societies. In the case of human societies, duality develops through a delicate balance between the order provided by the obligation to obey the law, and the freedom granted by individual and collective rights. For order to be maintained, there needs to be balance among the higher powers within society (represented by regulatory institutions), just as it is necessary for the group to perceive a certain degree of legitimacy in these powers. That balance can be lost in several scenarios, either by loss of legitimacy of the higher power, or when there are changes in the power and/or capabilities of the individuals that make up the social group.

Now, higher power is not always exercised by democratic regulatory institutions; it can also be exercised by a despot. Despotism can even alter the collective culture, causing repression to become a social institution of its own. The ability to punish another is called coercive power and is only possible when there is great asymmetry in the distribution of power. Coercive power requires energy to maintain it, creates resentment, and is not as well accepted by the masses as the power of reward (in which one can reward another). The power of reward produces greater obedience, but also requires resources. Similarly, both the power of reward and coercive power imply the ability to influence the masses and deactivate them.

In short, order is usually maintained in one of two ways: by an overwhelming force greater than that of the rest of society, or by the balance that can be achieved through consensus.[139]

---

139. "Obedience, Power, and Leadership – Principles of

The irony is that consensus can also be achieved by imposition; in this regard, it is worth noting that dictatorships usually end up losing any perception of legitimacy. This loss of legitimacy occurs when society realizes that the damage caused to any of its members or to society in general outweighs the benefits provided by the regime in terms of maintaining order.

When all is said and done, democracy comes the closest to maintaining order through a balance of forces. In a democracy, institutional mechanisms are created to maintain order and provide the option of changing a leader for one who will do a better job. It also provides a control platform to avoid dependence on a single omnipotent dictator who can harm a particular group or suck up all the resources to the detriment of the entire society.

Regardless of whether we are discussing dictatorships or democracies, something that we can observe in all human societies is that power is dynamic, and periodically recalibrated. The recalibration of power produces conflicts, which in turn help define the recalibration of the distribution of social power.

Usually, complex and rapid social changes require a "firm hand" phase, which allows order to be maintained during the transition in institutions. After a controlled transition process, a more equitable system can come into place, if the new institutions have been consolidated.

Social Psychology – 1st International Edition." 2014. Open-textbc.Ca. September 26, 2014. https://opentextbc.ca/socialpsychology/chapter/obedience-power-and-leadership/.

The concept of using a firm hand does not apply only to national governments. In fact, non-governmental social organisms such as religions can also have vertical structures, to which the different political theories can be applied.

Of course, it comes as no surprise that there are multiple instances in history where the transition has not been carried out properly. To give just one example, an uprising as violent as the French Revolution began with a social movement that used as its motto "Liberté, égalité, fraternité", an appeal to the most intrinsic and essential form of our social nature as human beings: the egalitarian societies of hunters and gatherers. The principle was fine but lacked sufficient social control mechanisms to allow the orderly transition of its institutions.

On the other hand, it is to be expected that in well-organized societies with an established order, such as those found in Europe, there is more space for equity as an essential human characteristic. However, in major territorial extensions with a lower level of organization, such as Russia or China, more authoritarian systems of government are required to maintain relative cohesion, peace and order.

Now, a curious fact is that social tranquility is not maintained only by the balance between citizen participation and system complexity. The economic situation plays a key role. As far back as the middle ages, Ibn Khaldun had already observed how economic growth and health numb a society and keep it at peace. He mentioned that luxuries destroy the collective sentiment and cause nations to be unable to defend themselves, so that they are absorbed by other nations. Meekness and docility lead to a lack of control and authority in the system. When a society is wild and not meek, it expands and absorbs other nations. It was already recognized at that time that religion allowed wild nations in conflict to submit to an authority, which would not be possible otherwise.

While not wishing to delve into the sphere of religious debate, it should be mentioned that there are historians who consider that when St. Augustine succeeded in promoting the belief that the goal of earthly life was to suffer in order to reach the city of God, it produced such meekness that mankind had a technological setback that lasted at least a thousand years (perhaps we are still feeling the consequences of this setback).

So, we already know what can cause one nation fall into the hands of another. But ... what makes one nation try to take control of another? Is there something else going on in the mind of those complex primates of the human variety? Apparently, there is. If we look carefully at history, imperialism emerges as an exaltation of nationalism, or as a perception of being the only ones with a handle on religious or moral truth. There are combinations of the two, which in many cases can affect the expansion of a nation's free trade area (by including more territory and population that consumes and produces). Commercial imperialism often goes hand in hand with foreign policy formulated to promote the country's transnationals. Governments can support the expansion their national companies using the same arguments made for territorial imperialism. Any expansion is maintained to the point where the cost of expanding (including monetary costs, but also costs in maintaining order) exceeds the benefits in resources.

In short... a story of the meek being controlled and the wild doing the controlling. What would Marx think of this whole mess? The truth is that in human societies a small group of people have control of production, corporations, private foundations, universities, political parties, high public decision-making positions, and the means of communication. That group, called the "elite", understands a pyramidal structure of power within society, and contrary to what the conspiracy theorists proclaim, they are respectful of laws, freedoms and rights; at least this is usually the case in Western democracies. Many of their members come into the world as heirs, but they are usually open as a group to those who share their principles, beliefs and attitudes, and want to join. The elite often maintain close cooperation marked by social cohesion, since they live in the same places, read the same magazines and newspapers, go to the same clubs, send their children to the same schools, attend the same churches, play together, and naturally, give preference to each other at the time of doing business and closing deals. This close coexistence and cooperation gives them a similar visions of things, including economics and politics.[140] Although it is disturbing to the masses that the decisions with the greatest social impact are taken by the few, their power increases as average citizens participate less, protest less, and think less.

---

140   "The Power Elite." 2019. Udel.Edu. 2019. https://www1.udel.edu/htr/Psc105/Texts/power.html.

Now, the big question is, why can't everyone become part of the elite, creating an egalitarian society where we share equally in the distribution of power? Would it be possible? Well, the answer is a bit tricky. Evidence shows that throughout history, expansion of the social elite leads to greater competition within the elite, as well as stimulating the emergence of new candidates for the elite, usually with a lot of education and ability. Historically, the elite's enlargement usually coincides with the moments of greatest social inequality, leading to ideological polarization, and fragmentation and instability of the political class. This phenomenon can lead to revolutions and even wars, as demonstrated by the American Civil War or the Russian Revolution. In other words, if you want to destabilize a human society, enlarge your elite without restraint. If social violence is to be avoided, there must be cooperation within the elite, a strengthening of laws, and an understanding of social inequities.

Speaking of political instability and conflicts: While a conflict is essentially a psychological confrontation to undermine the opponent's calculations and self-confidence, we cannot ignore the exchange of physical damage that inflicts even greater injury during a conflict. The most violent examples of conflicts between humans are wars, which have become increasingly violent thanks to our ingenuity and technological progress as a species. The level of violence in wars has been steadily increasing since the Iron Age when developments in manufacturing led to the production of more lethal weaponry. Such fabrications have been used not only in armed conflicts, but for hunting and agriculture as well. This makes it clear why the industrial powers have restricted the transfer of technology to other less developed countries: industrialization implies scientific, technological and logistical developments that could be used for the manufacture of more lethal weapons that would threaten the established order.

Let us not forget that despite all the psychological manipulation and violence inherent to conflicts, their final objective is not military but political (referring to the distribution of social power). The military aspect is only one variable among many in the equation. More recently, social networks have come to play an important role along with other forms of cyberspace communication, demonstrating great effectiveness in achieving psychological objectives in public opinion battles. Their great effectiveness leads to the suggestion that they could replace weapons to some extent in certain types of conflicts.

In the end, all public opinion battles end up focusing on the fact that humans make decisions based on beliefs and emotions rather than on concrete scientific knowledge or factual evidence, which can distance us from reality and produce social and/or economic distortions. It is for this reason that political debate has been trending towards a more temperamental, emotional and dogmatic style, versus a more rational rhetoric.

If there is something difficult in this life, it is making good decisions. Making decisions almost always implies consequences, but bad decisions always imply regrettable consequences. Political decision-making relies on an overlap of disciplines such as mathematics, sociology, psychology, economics and political science, among others, all of which are increasingly studied with greater sophistication for this purpose. Decisions are also made by calculating the possible risk they entail, which depends to a large extent on the level of certainty of obtaining the expected result. The weighing of risks acquired greater relevance in decision-making following the First World War, when psychologists, sociologists, anthropologists, and biologists converged to study cooperation among individuals within a group. They found that decisions made emotionally defy the evidence, and in times of crisis, are often made when arguments cannot be reviewed.[141]

Subjectivity not only affects public opinion; it also affects the actions of politicians. That is why politicians need to seek a balance between realism and idealism, and establish priorities based on the effectiveness of the policy in obtaining a desired effect.

Desired effect... subjectivity... politicians... this whole subject is taking on another nuance. Apparently, our ancestors - and our primate family - are gradually turning into modern politicians. Or perhaps little by little our politicians are drawing closer to the circle of chimpanzees divvying up tasty morsels of meat. The truth is that political struggles, organized into political parties in human societies, usually have their roots in something related to our own evolution: our brain. Our survival instinct also plays a role. This discussion is precisely the subject of the next chapter.

---

141. "A Brief History of Decision Making." 2014. Harvard Business Review. August 2014. https://hbr.org/2006/01/a-brief-history-of-decision-making.

VIII. Evolutionary foundations of conservatism and liberalism

Let's forget about economic models for a moment and concentrate on the eternal dilemma of the struggle between order imposed by authority, and equity within a group. The analysis of any political scheme requires that we establish the evolutionary and neuroscientific basis of conservatism and liberalism.

Time and again, it can be observed that human beings tend to polarize politically into at least two groups, with different names given to each variant according to the political culture.

In this chapter, we will conduct a rudimentary dichotomization of political currents, classifying them into two large groups. We will label one group Conservatism, and the other, Liberalism. Regardless of whether we are talking about a socialist, communist, capitalist or any other economy, irrespective of the economic ideology behind the political groups, and notwithstanding the core ideology, there is usually a more conservative group and a more liberal one.

As stated in previous chapters, this whole convolution involves multiple disciplines, among which the application of the neurosciences to politics cannot be overlooked. Neuropolitics, as this field is called, allows us to understand a little more about neuronal interactions and brain functions around certain behaviors related to access to power.

The first (conservative) group corresponds to the imprint of our common ancestor, which leads us to identify some external threat to our social group and clearly react as primates, in the sense of developing cohesion to organize and support a strong leader (alpha male) to defend the group from the perceived external threat.

The second group corresponds to the nature of Homo sapiens, which can be observed in groups of hunters. Here, a balance tends to be maintained through an equitable system with a solid social contract that guarantees the elimination of any group member seeking to position himself as the alpha male or abuse the group in some way.

Liberals and conservatives will never agree, illustrating the eternal political ideological division within human societies.

Thus, we can identify a liberal group - usually labeled "the left" - as one that challenges the "ruling" power with the intention of changing a hierarchical system for one that is more equitable, usually involving the removal of the social elite. In contrast, a right-wing group generally advocates to uphold the existing hierarchical order, but with strong leadership to maintain internal order and prevent the group's decline through internal conflicts, or to defend the group against an external threat.

Under such different values, a wide range of political interests are usually aligned, including economic and moral interests, as well as the degree of intervention that is expected to be exercised by the State.

The big question is how individual affinity for a particular point of view or political leaning is determined. Is it a phenomenon rooted in genetics, or is it something merely learned? Well, that depends on the age of the individual. There is a study showing that political attitudes in adolescents and young adults are more likely to be swayed by various environmental factors. In mature adults, however, the genetic influence becomes evident, and will remain so the rest of their lives.[142]

So, let's talk about the characteristics of ideological extremes, keeping in mind that in between are found countless shades of grey and that this where most individuals in a society fall.

Conservatives

The fact is that there is a large group of political scientists and political psychologists who agree that liberals and conservatives differ in their political positions because of their personal, psychological, and even genetic differences. Conservatives appear to be more reactive to

---

142   "Differences in Conservative and Liberal Brains - 2016 Presidential Election - ProCon.Org." n.d. 2016election. Procon.Org. Accessed July 14, 2020. http://2016election. procon.org/view.resource.php?resourceID=005927.

negative environmental stimuli such as threats, causing them to think in terms of strengthening the military and the laws, stopping immigration, promoting the availability of weapons, etc., all because of a biology aimed at responding quickly and forcefully to any threat. Conservatism seems to correspond biologically to a greater desire for order, structure, closure, certainty, consistency, simplicity and familiarity, as well as to a greater perception of danger, sensitivity to threats and anxiety in the face of death. Despite this profile, there is scientific evidence that suggests that liberals tend to be more neurotic and that conservatives tend to experience more happiness and satisfaction in life, implying that stability could be an important factor in human happiness.[143]

This whole theory and the ideology it generates appear to be deeply connected to biological defense mechanisms against threats in the environment. There are studies showing that conservative (right-wing) ideology is related to a greater negative response to disgusting images or threatening conditions, as well as a greater response to sudden noises. The difference is so great that when two images are placed side-by-side, one pleasant and the other unpleasant, conservatives spend more time looking and reacting to the unpleasant image, while liberals spend more time looking at the pleasant one. These findings seem linked to a greater tendency

---

143   Mooney, Chris. n.d. "Scientists Are Beginning to Figure out Why Conservatives Are...conservative." Mother Jones. http://www.motherjones.com/politics/2014/07/biology-ideology-john-hibbing-negativity-bias.

among conservatives to safeguard purity and morality as part of a political mindset.

Another interesting study found that it is easier for liberals to direct their gaze in the direction that other people are looking, suggesting that conservatives tend to be more individualistic and difficult to influence. Such individualism could explain why conservatives advocate paying less tax to finance subsidies and social assistance to the less fortunate.

Oddly enough, four separate studies have suggested that conservatism is supported by a form of reasoning based on the principal of least effort. We know that humans are a social species and that we tend to believe what we are told[144] as a way of complying with this principle. Developing critical thinking not only requires humility, it also requires greater effort and a greater expenditure of time and energy to verify the source and compare it with the information provided by other sources.

An important question is, can an educational system that promotes "beliefs" instead of critical analysis be a breeding ground for conservatives? Likewise, if populists use demagogy to show that simple answers solve complex multidimensional problems, do these approaches attract the conservative vote more easily than any complex approach to problem solving?

So, we see that there are differences in terms of interest in analyzing and verifying information,

---

144   "Critical Thinking in a Post-Truth Era." 2017. Penguin Random House Common Reads. March 22, 2017. http://commonreads.com/2017/03/22/daniel-j-levitin-critical-thinking/.

but... What about controlling a situation? We all feel at some point that we lose control over the situation, be it cancer, death, love, or natural or economic disasters, for example. The feeling of not being in control leads to fear (everyone who has boarded a plane knows how it feels to cross through an area of turbulence). That is the same fear that causes us to make decisions without thinking, and the same fear that leads us to superstition.

The perception of security depends on how much control we think we have over the situation, how much margin of error we have, and how terrible the consequences could be. The more fear there is, the greater will be the desired margin between the individual and the damage caused by the potential threat.

Decisions based on fear often lack adequate analysis, opening the door for the creation of a market in which profit can be made from superstition. New offers of services appear around fear or the lack of control of a situation, such as a cure for incurable diseases, magical solutions to love disappointments, spells, exorcisms, etc. The core of the superstition market is to give the false idea that control of an out-of-control situation can be regained, all within a context of power dynamics.

Clearly, not all rituals and beliefs are superstitions. The magical properties we give them make them superstitions. Individuals with obsessive-compulsive traits tend to have more rituals and give more importance to them, which can be confused with superstitious behavior. Those who are more exposed to superstitious beliefs include people who experience high levels of anxiety, sleep disorders, excessive worry, obsessive thoughts, or simple exhaustion. Belief in a false certainty is better than no certainty at all. Superstition seems to be more common in women, probably because in the modern world, women tend to rely more on external factors for their success while men tend to perceive that they have greater control over their future.[145]

It is not only women who are more superstitious: so are people with a tendency to depression, or anyone who feels they are unable to control important aspects of their environment.[146]

Experimental psychologist Bruce Hood told TIME magazine that the human brain is designed to believe in superstitions as part of the need for patterns and order in the environment. There is a tendency to give supernatural qualities to anything we cannot understand. Superstition cannot be framed exclusively in religion, and we experience it from the time we are children when we imagine the monsters under the bed, or behind the door, or everything that can appear in the dark. From early in life it is common for humans to endow inanimate objects with supernatural properties.[147]

---

145 Albert, Sarah. n.d. "The Psychology of Superstition." WebMD. Accessed July 14, 2020. http://www.webmd.com/mental-health/features/psychology-of-superstition#1.
146 September 2013, Marc Lallanilla 13. n.d. "Friday the 13th: Why Humans Are So Superstitious." Livescience.Com. http://www.livescience.com/39566-friday-the-13th-superstitions.html.
147 *Cruz, Gilbert. "Why We're Superstitious." Time. Time Inc., April 10, 2009. http://content.time.com/time/arts/article/0,8599,1890165,00.html.*

We can also observe superstition in skeptics and atheists, revealed by the need to believe in something "super" natural, such as aliens, the super-beings behind conspiracy theories, the magical powers of people, objects or substances, magical creatures, and—why not?—even the United Nations' secret plan to homosexualize humanity or control the world population.

Now, this book is about primates and politics. The topic of superstition is touched upon here because religion not only accommodates superstition, but also factors into politics (understanding politics as the science of competing in the race for power), often in association with conservatism.

Liberals

Having already reviewed the profile for conservative thinking, it is much easier to understand the liberal mindset.

It is common knowledge that in any human society, an individual who harms another member of the group is usually shunned and/or punished. It is not surprising, therefore, that one of the political groups will tend to serve as a cohesive force to unite those most interested in protecting the weakest from the harm that the strongest within society can do to them. From this idea, you can understand why liberals often challenge the dominant power, since they tend to give priority to protecting the underdog.

Here's an interesting point to consider: If liberals are supposedly less reactive and more capable of dealing with complex situations, does this mean that an individual's mentality can be made more liberal by teaching them to deal with complex situations? The question arises because it would be interesting to determine whether creative individuals trained to deal with complex concepts such as music, dance, painting and other art forms, become politically liberal. If the answer were affirmative, it would make perfect sense that the emergence of political and economic liberalism coincided with the classical period of music, dance, literature and the visual arts. Now, this may raise another question: Do the simplest and least complex expressions of art, such as certain repetitive and redundant forms of electronic music, make individuals less able to adapt to change and easier to manipulate based on fear or the simplicity posed by populism?

Contrasts between liberals and conservatives

Without a doubt, there are significant differences between the mindset and views of conservatives and liberals. In fact, we can list situations in which there would be an important contrast between the brain responses of conservatives and liberals. But why would there be two such different mentalities in the same species? What happened along the path of evolution?

Apparently, conservatism implies an evolutionary advantage. It is easy to see how feeling fear more readily and having greater reactive responses to change or to the presence of a potential threat would have given evolutionary advantages to our ancestors living in the Pleistocene (Homo habilis or Homo erectus).

Liberalism, on the other hand, seems more advantageous in the face of changing conditions due to climatic shifts, which apparently put great pressure on our species and forced us to become what we are today. Liberalism also seems to provide an evolutionary advantage in the face of today's growing social and technological complexity.

There is a neuropolitics study that found that American conservatives tend to be more structured and persistent in their judgments. Now, it is also true that political positions are not exclusive to a specific ideological current. Political positions can vary depending on the subject, and the spectrum in each situation includes the entire scale of gray between black and white. In addition to the variations in political position depending on the problem being confronted, there are also differences in the way the brain itself works. For example, it has been observed that liberals experience four to nine times more electrical brain activity when dealing with conflicts, which can make them more inclined to engage in violent confrontation. This greater electrical activity could also be part of the reason liberals tend to support revolutions more readily, including scientific revolutions and new concepts. In short, while liberals are more at ease dealing with change, conservatives tend to block additional information that might distract them, which can be an advantage or disadvantage depending on the situation.[148]

---

148   "Success A Family Affair? Willingness To Take Risks And Trust Others Are Inherited, Study Suggests." n.d. ScienceDaily. Accessed July 14, 2020. https://www.sciencedaily.com/releases/2006/11/061128140652.htm.

Personality factors can also hinder change. For example, neurotic individuals see threats everywhere, making change stressful for them. The same can be said of those who are unable to deal with ambiguity or lack of control. Personality traits that have been identified as predictive factors for resistance to change include the need for a stable routine, stress, short-term thinking, and cognitive stiffness or dogmatism. In the end, human beings tend to be ambivalent about change, although there will be those who assimilate change more readily than others.[149]

Fear as a factor related to political preference is perfectly illustrated by a study that found that both liberals and conservatives respond in a similar way to positive stimuli, but that conservatives are more sensitive to negative stimuli. Another study found that conservatives focus on avoiding negative results, while liberals tend to focus on moving towards positive results.

But if we are going to talk about beliefs in politics, would it surprise you to learn that the same word can have different meanings according to the individual's political beliefs? Apparently, conservatives and liberals have different patterns of word association.[150] In fact, a

---

149   *2017. [online] Available at: <https://www.psy-chologytoday.com/intl/blog/sideways-view/201610/resistance-change%20(accessed%202017) > [Accessed 10 November 2017].*

150   Li, P. 2017. Review of *Speaking Two Languages in America: A Semantic Space Analysis of How Presiden-tial Candidates and Their Supporters Represent Abstract Political Concepts Differently. Behav Res Methods*, no. doi: 10.3758/s13428-017-0931-5. (July).

clear example of these differences in association about word meaning can be found in the word "gender." For liberals, the word "gender" is immediately associated with the fight for freedom and social equity, while for conservatives, it is associated with social changes that can shake the way society has been understood for generations, and can even be seen as a threat to the reproduction of descendants.

This is because the human brain processes information economically to obtain the solution to problems. Without a doubt, efficiency is part of nature, of evolution, and of our own brain, where the principle of least effort prevails. Like biological systems, our brain is efficient and economical, using the least amount of resources to think (not to mention that it is even cheaper not to think). As not all brains work the same, we are still a long way from understanding all the implications of the concept, which opens the door to new research.[151]

Elite theory

Without a doubt, one of the issues that has received the most attention in the different political currents has to do with the way in which wealth is interpreted and acquired.

The renowned elite theory speaks of solidarity and collaboration among a small group of individuals who share much in common and have access to many

---

151   "Human Brain Applies Law Of Least Effort When Solving Problems." 2016. Scienceagogo.Com. 2016. http://www.scienceagogo.com/news/20000520165209data_trunc_sys.shtml.

more resources than the rest of the population. Can this acquisition of wealth be associated with liberalism or conservatism? It's hard to say. Among the elite you will find all kinds of interesting mixtures of liberal and conservative ideas, but these differences in political ideology do not seem to be at all relevant. What does appear to be more consistent is the concept that the best and correct way to access resources in society is through the established order. But of course, how could it be otherwise? It is precisely the elite that are best adapted to access resources, and in the best position to play by the existing rules.

I take this opportunity to share an anecdote which left me with many questions but helped me to see how the understanding of finance can vary among individuals. In my year of rural internship as a doctor I had the opportunity to play monopoly with two 8-year-old children who were hospitalized, but I decided it would be better to observe them without taking part. One was from the Ngöbe-Buglé ethnic group (an indigenous group from western Panama); the other was from a mestizo village. It is worth noting that in 2015, the Ngöbe-Buglé had a poverty index of 98% according to the United Nations Development Program (UNDP). The mestizo boy quickly began buying up properties from the onset of the game. The Ngöbe boy held on to his money and did not buy any property until he realized his mistake, but it was too late. The Ngöbe-Buglé region has 6,968 square kilometers and a population of 154,355 inhabitants. Although its soils are not the most fertile, it has beautiful mountain landscapes, extensive primary forests and pristine beaches. Its main downfall is its low level of human development. Questions arise from that monopoly game: Could it be that the awareness of being less developed (individually or collectively) than others makes an individual (or group) less willing to take risks? And does this lack of self-confidence distance such people from leadership positions within a society, a country, or even the global economy? Might this be the principle behind the elite theory? Scholars on the subject assert that those who lead in society are more generous, supportive and inclined to take risks. Perhaps it is this willingness to take risks and part with money that causes a certain group of individuals to quickly increase their wealth, while others like the Ngöbe-Buglé are immersed in a spiral of poverty.

We know that economic success goes hand in hand with ease of taking risks. This behavior can be a developed through practice so that it becomes increasingly more natural for an individual, but it has also been found to be transmitted within families. A person who takes risks easily is more likely to join up with other people who are comfortable taking risks, leading to the creation of economic groups as well as consolidating families in an advantageous economic position. The question remains: Is taking risks transmitted in families because it is learned from childhood, or through genetics? Both factors probably play a role. There may be a greater genetic propensity to take risks, and at the same time there may be learning and development of such behavior.

Information management

When we integrate cognitive, emotional and motivational processes, and mix these together with rigid beliefs, worldviews and emotions, psychological barriers appear that give us a skewed and distorted idea of information. These same socio-psychological barriers can become obstacles for the assimilation of new information and provide fodder for all kinds of conflicts, including armed. Likewise, these obstacles can become the greatest enemy of peace processes.[152] Beliefs can hinder the influence of information on human reasoning in multiple issues, such as medical treatments, vaccines, reforms to educational programs, actions in the economy, changes in traffic, migration, and... the list could go on and on with examples from different contexts of daily life. It is clear that people must be equipped with information and skills to overcome these barriers, even in such basic aspects as teaching people to eat healthy and do physical activity.[153] However, a vicious cycle is created when a belief barrier causes a person to shut out new information, information that could provide precisely the opportunity to overcome the barrier that truncates the individual's ability to reason.

152   "PIJ.ORG: Societal Beliefs and Emotions as Socio-Psychological Barriers to Peaceful Conflict Resolution By Daniel Bar-Tal and Eran Halperin." n.d. PIJ.ORG. Accessed July 14, 2020. http://www.pij.org/details.php?id=1535.
153   Ross, Anna. 2015. Review of *Beliefs as Barriers to Healthy Eating and Physical Activity*. *Australian Journal of Psychology*, no. DOI: 10.1111/ajpy.12103 (September). https://doi.org/10.1111/ajpy.12103.

How to deal with these barriers is a question that will likely continue to insert itself into our politics and contribute to the replacement of partisan policy based on arguments with the populism induced by current political marketing (in which all electoral options end up resembling each other).

Another bias in information management occurs when we have information gaps. Gaps can also help create barriers to reasoning, as our brain tends to fill in the blanks where information is missing. The way our brain fills in these empty spaces has been widely studied, and can be observed, for example, in our vision: we all have a blind spot in our visual field, but we are not aware of it because the brain fills it in. And while vision may be the best-studied example, our brain seems to easily construct missing information and fill in the empty spaces in many aspects of thinking.[154]

To fill in these information gaps, the brain draws from the material immediately surrounding the void. It can be said that our individual experiences are largely illusions, where we see very little and create the rest. [155]Is this the reason why it is so easy to spread false information on social networks, taking advantage of the information gaps in public opinion? One thing is certain: when good communication is absent from

---

154 "Trinicenter.Com - Discovery Shows How Brain 'Fills In Blanks' To Help Us See." n.d. Www.Trinicenter.Com. http://www.trinicenter.com/more/HowBrainFillsInBlanks.htm.

155 Ramachandran, Vilayanur S., and Diane Rogers-Ramachandran. 2005. "Mind the Gap." *Scientific American Mind* 16 (1): 100–198. https://doi.org/10.1038/scientificamericanmind0405-100.

politics and not enough information is provided to the population, peoples' brains will fill in the blanks, be it with beliefs, prejudices, false information, or the natural tendency to fill the void with the information that surrounds it.

Brain hemispheres

There is a myth that political affinity depends on which hemisphere of the brain is the most developed in an individual. The human brain has two hemispheres, right and left. The right is associated with creativity and the left with speech and mathematical ability. Proponents of this myth correlate the creative function of the right hemisphere with liberalism, while the language function of the left hemisphere is associated more closely with conservatism. Such thinking may be the product of studies like the one that found liberals to be more creative and conservatives more organized. However, the difference between the two hemispheres is not as marked as has been believed. The predominance of one hemisphere or the other, as well as how they work together, can be studied in individuals whose brain hemispheres have been disconnected as part of a surgical treatment for epilepsy. This allows for a comparison of the way the brain works in individuals with separate hemispheres as opposed to healthy individuals whose two hemispheres are fully connected and working together. These studies have found that the theoretical distinction between the cerebral hemispheres ignores the fact that there are many different types of creativity.

Thus, the left hemisphere can invent stories to explain what the right hemisphere creates.[156]

In these studies of patients with surgically disconnected brain hemispheres, it was found that the hemispheres can function independently when they lose the ability to communicate. This independent functioning can reach the point where the two hemispheres give antagonistic signals, such as when one hand tries to stop what the other hand is doing.

It should be mentioned that this myth is not completely without merit. We know that the left hemisphere of the brain has more dopamine receptors (a neurotransmitter), while the right hemisphere has more norepinephrine receptors (another neurotransmitter). Norepinephrine increases our response to unusual stimuli and facilitates our selective attention. It can be said that the right hemisphere enjoys change, making new connections and analyzing multiple possible meanings for each change, while the left hemisphere struggles with change as it lacks the ability to make a comprehensive analysis or relate different pieces of information to each other. The left hemisphere processes information in a more monosemantic sense while the right hemisphere can work with more ambiguous concepts. Because of this, the left hemisphere tends to limit analytical results to predetermined parameters.[157]

156   "Why the Left-Brain Right-Brain Myth Will Probably Never Die." n.d. Psychology Today. Accessed July 14, 2020. https://www.psychologytoday.com/blog/brain-myths/201206/why-the-left-brain-right-brain-myth-will-probably-never-die.
157   "Neuropolitics.Org - Neuropolitics Resources

From the preceding paragraphs, it might seem logical to conclude that individuals with a more highly developed right brain would tend to sympathize more with liberal groups, while those with greater development of the left hemisphere would identify more with conservatives, not as an economic or ideological current but as a way to avoid changes that produce confusion and imply a greater expenditure of energy to understand and adapt. But is this true? Does greater development of a particular hemisphere determine affinity for a particular political current? If not, why is the myth of hemispheric development so widely discussed? The simple truth is that both hemispheres can sympathize with different aspects of different political ideological currents. These currents include multiple positions on many social problems, where each solution proposed may relate more to the development of one hemisphere or the other.

Limbic system

Fear is an evolutionary advantage inherent to the survival instinct that prevailed among primates because of the constant threat to reproduction (conflict with other males or females), need to escape from predators, etc. In short, evolution has been honing our survival instinct over the course of 600 million years. We all feel fear at some point in life, but what makes those hair-raising emotions surface? Well, past emotions and the memories

and Information." n.d. Www.Neuropolitics.Org. http://www.neuropolitics.org/Conservative-Left-Brain-Liberal-Right-Brain.htm.

we associate with them play a big part, but there are also three errors that can trigger fear: over-estimation of the threat, under-estimation of opportunities, and under-valuing available resources.[158]

In short, all those emotions and fears have their reason for being, and their explanation. We just need to explore certain parts of our brain a little.

The limbic system is a set of structures located around the vital centers of our brain. It plays an important role in memory and emotions. Among these structures is the hypothalamus, the hippocampus, and the amygdala. The hypothalamus regulates basic functions such as blood pressure, heart rate, respiratory rate, digestion, and sweating, among others, while the hippocampus appears to be related to long-term memory.

The amygdala, which occupies a small space in the temporal lobe, is associated with fear and repression of actions that may endanger us. The amygdala shares characteristics with the hemisphere in which it is found. The left amygdala will cause us to fear verbal concepts, while the right amygdala is more related to anxiety and fear of environmental changes.

The amygdala is a structure with a key function in political science. The lack of function of the amygdala can cause a mouse to openly challenge a cat to a fight, in the same way that a dictator of a small country can provoke a war with a military superpower, for want of

---

158   "What Makes You Feel Threatened?" n.d. Psychology Today. Accessed July 14, 2020. https://www.psychology-today.com/blog/your-wise-brain/201601/what-makes-you-feel-threatened.

diplomacy. What might seem to be madness could in fact be underexpression of the amygdala.

The cingulum is an area closely tied to the limbic system. It helps us focus attention on important moments for our emotions and is related to the sensation of pain. Scientific studies have suggested that the cingulate cortex detects conflicts and induces adaptive control of behavior. From these findings, it has been proposed that this function demonstrates the connection between nonhuman and human primates, since its damage produces similar behavioral consequences in both groups. The functions observed for the cingulum also help to explain context-dependent learning and behavior control. [159]The anterior cingulum has been linked to tolerance of uncertainty and appears to be more developed in people with liberal tendencies, making them more tolerant of conflicts and change.

The insular cortex is another area linked to the limbic system, connecting it to the neocortex. It has been associated with multiple functions, including abstract thinking and rapid decision making. It seems to play an important role in integrating the information gathered by our senses with our emotions. There is scientific evidence that when faced with dangerous conditions, liberal-minded individuals have more activity in the left insular cortex, while those identifying as conservatives have more activity in the right amygdala.

---

159   Mansouri, Farshad. n.d. Review of *Monitoring Demands for Executive Control: Shared Functions between Human and Nonhuman Primates. Trends in Neurosciences* 40 (1): 15–27. Accessed July 14, 2020. https://doi.org/ https://doi.org/10.1016/j.tins.2016.11.001.

All of these interactions between the different parts of our brain are brought into balance through a process that involves the development of the cerebral hemispheres, amygdalas, our memories and past experiences, generating a result that will define our location on that grayscale between purely liberal and purely conservative.

At the end of the day, it is the moderates on the gray scale who define elections by moving towards one side of the balance or the other.

It is worth asking how this distribution of balance between conservatives and liberals behaves in the general population. Well, there is no universal answer. Surely, the genetics of the population (studies in different countries have found that around 40% of political tendency is hereditary)[160] and the history of each nation, as well as the events experienced by each generation, will change the point of equilibrium. According to data gathered by Gallup for the United States, the distribution among the different political tendencies has remained relatively stable in the last 20 years, with approximately 20% liberal, 37% moderate, and 40% conservative, including 9% who identify as hardline liberal and 21% who identify as hardline conservative.

It appears that liberals experience greater activity in the insular cortex and the anterior cingulum of the cerebral cortex (both areas are responsible for dealing

160.September 2016, Adam Hadhazy 29. n.d. "Life's Extremes: Democrat vs. Republican." Livescience.Com. http://www.livescience.com/17534-life-extremes-democrat-republican.html.

with conflicting information), while conservatives tend to have a larger and more developed amigdala, the center of fear. All this helps us to understand why liberals seem to have a greater tolerance for the uncertainty inherent to gray-scale political positions, while conservatives tend to adopt more rigid black-or-white stances.

When seeking to answer questions such as: Who are we? How did we get to this point? Why are we the way we are, and why do we behave the way do from day to day in the face of different natural phenomena, including social ones? ...we come to the inevitable realization that there is vast evidence of our origins and our essence, and that the examples of our nature could fill volumes. The next chapter is a compilation of some of those examples.

IX. Evolutionary theory of politics: evidence and applications

This book is born precisely from a bibliographic review based on a specific event: the election of Donald Trump as President of the United States in November 2016. Throughout this journey, we have been moving steadily back to where it all began—with concrete facts. We must understand that all political analysis can be interpreted from the perspective of conservation of the individual, the group, and the species. Politics is part of us, and the way it is conducted is also a product of our own evolution as a species.

More than 6 months before the U.S. elections in November 2016, Scott Adams, the creator of "Dilbert", said that having nothing to lose increased Donald Trump's chance of winning, since it opened the door to rhetorical discourse. The then candidate was clear on never proposing an analysis of the country's problems and focusing the entire campaign on appealing to emotions, which represent 90% of the decision-making process of voters. Trump employed two clear persuasion techniques with lethal precision: 1. use an unusual lexicon in politics, and 2. relate your statement to the subject's physical appearance (in order to create a visual association, which makes it easy to remember what was said). The best persuasion tool used by Trump was to create for himself the identity of the alpha male, while Clinton had to settle for the sympathy of vulnerable groups.[161]

The unexpected result raised other questions, such as: Why did the West's "model" democracy choose a president who projects a somewhat authoritarian style? Trump never showed a deep mastery of the problems of the State, selling himself instead as a figure determined to solve certain issues even if by force, a force reminiscent of the alpha male in a troop of chimpanzees.

We saw from our review of the first human societies that their behavior was not comparable to that of chimpanzees. Instead, these early societies were small, egalitarian groups of hunter-gatherers. Chimpanzees, on the other hand, may have retained more social features of our common ancestor. With time, science will provide the answer.

---

161. Riffs, Michael Cavna /artist for Comic, Covering Visual Storytelling, Cartoon Art/Illustration, comedy/satire, and animationWriter/critic. n.d. "Donald Trump Will Win in a Landslide. *The Mind behind 'Dilbert' Explains Why." Washington Post. Accessed July 14, 2020. https://www.washingtonpost.com/news/comic-riffs/wp/2016/03/21/donald-trump-will-win-in-a-landslide-the-mind-behind-dilbert-explains-why/?utm_term=.bd2fff67a1f3.

Evolutionary theory of politics

The fact is that a review of history reveals a curious cycle between equitable societies and authoritarianism, from which I propose what I call in this book the "evolutionary theory of politics."

In practical terms, it seems that every time a society feels that the political or social situation is getting out of control, they: 1. seek more authoritarian leaders, and 2. seek a reduction in the level of social complexity. The triumph of Donald Trump in 2016 is a good example of the first tendency, while the United Kingdom's departure from the European community, also remembered as "Brexit", illustrates the second. It can be said that Brexit was a vote against the changes that were occurring in the United Kingdom, which were happening at a faster rate than at least half of the population (those who voted to leave the union) was able to assimilate.

From the first hunter-gatherer societies we can deduce that humans do not like authoritarian leaders, perhaps because of the risk that such figures will take advantage of their greater access to resources (remember that reciprocal altruism requires a lot of trust in order to be sustainable over time). However, there are circumstances in which the collective preference turns to authoritarianism, which makes us wonder whether verticalization in human social structures (towards authoritarianism) as part of a repetitive cycle is the result of increasing social complexity and the desire to maintain order. Or perhaps it is the other way around, and the order imposed by a single strong authority is what produces increased levels of complexity. It is true that strong leaders often institute changes that bring progress, but it is also true that in the face of increased social complexity, lack of order leads to collapse.

The United States has been a relatively equitable society that began its expansion with strong institutions, but under the authority of England. During this colonial period, England had sufficient military capacity to maintain order. Following the independence of the United States, the strength of the previously established institutions enabled a gradual growth in the complexity of the nation while maintaining order within a relatively equitable system.

Cycles of authoritarianism alternated with egalitarianism seem to be so important when contemplating any change in a human society that multiple historical errors can be observed when they are not considered. For example, when these cycles were ignored by key U.S. foreign policy decision makers, the country ended up with wars in Iraq and Syria. Both wars can be considered tactical errors, because before you can bring "egalitarianism" to a society, it must first have the necessary institutional structures for maintaining peace and order. You cannot establish egalitarianism in a milieu where order depends on a single person who is precisely the target of elimination. The organization of institutions requires an extensive process of social organization which cannot be imposed from the outside, much less through war.

It is interesting to note that a dictatorship can lead to a revolution that takes one of three paths:

1. It can lead to disorder and a new vertical system, such as the "gangster capitalism" of today's Russia.

2. It can lead to disorder and a new dictatorship, as in the case of the French Revolution or the Arab Spring.

3. The only way the fall of a totalitarian system can lead to an inclusive democracy is when there has been institutional strengthening prior to the revolution, as was the case with the United States; the institutional mechanisms that guarantee compliance with the law were already in place.

An interesting transition might take place in China if its leaders fully embrace the need to change the system for the country to move forward. China's system is already more participatory than some democracies but continues to maintain a verticality of authority. This verticality could represent an advantage in achieving an orderly transition from a totalitarian system to an inclusive democracy, by promoting unity in a nation with a complex population, diversity and territorial extension.

Taking these elements into account, let's look at another political tactical failure: the Arab Spring in Egypt. The lack of clear institutions and participation and organization of civil society, as well as the lack of political pluralism, translated into the only possible outcome: the changing of one dictator for a similar system.

All of this can lead to the conclusion that neither post-Napoleonic France nor Germany after Hitler would have been able to move forward without the strength of their government systems to guarantee order and compliance with the law within their territories.

In the case of the European Union, on the other hand, we have a group of countries which, having achieved relatively sold institutions and an adequate culture of participation, face the challenge of integrating at a higher level of complexity. Their integration confronts significant obstacles that hamper progress due to a lack of clear authority. There is no firm hand to impose the order needed to drive the changes the region requires to maintain its competitiveness within the global geo-political order. This helps to explain why Catalonia's independence is unlikely to happen anytime soon.

Violence and Survival

So, what role does violence play in all this? Why the wars?

Interestingly, the international community itself behaves as a system of individuals (nations) with its own heterogeneity. As we have seen before, in human societies the individual who harms others without justification is never well viewed. This type of action can lead to violence. An example of the inclination of human groups towards violence was the Second World War. Without going into detail on the complex tangle of forces and motives that led to the confrontation, the invasion of Poland was the initial aggression by one individual (the German nation) towards another (the Polish nation). This was followed by a series of attacks by the same individual on other members of the community. These acts of aggression in the (international) community were rejected by the collective and led to the organization of the group (United Nations Organization) to establish norms and mechanisms to prevent similar events in the future.

Compared to the great conflicts that have developed in Europe, the situation in the Middle East is more complex. There is no unanimous position among the powers that control the geopolitical order with respect to the political condition of each country. Such divergence of interests between powers makes it difficult to impose order and instills antagonistic values, with points of view and ideologies that elude understanding.

Of course, for there to be large-scale violence there must be a balance of military capacity such that each of the parties involved believes it is able to win the conflict. Furthermore, the confrontation must generate a potential benefit greater than the resources that a war would entail. The Cold War is a clear example of the opposite; doubt as to the ability to defeat the other party and the very high cost that a conflict would have incurred (especially in terms of destruction) prevented an armed confrontation between the Communist bloc and the West. There were tense situations between the parties, with both sides sponsoring guerrilla warfare against the other, but without full-on conflict during the 40 years it lasted.

Another example is the Korean peninsula. Neither country can defeat the other, not because of their own military capacity but because of the support that both sides have on the part of decisive powers in the world order. The war has already taken place, and the measuring of forces ended up defining the "status quo" as the best alternative to a conflict in which neither party has a good chance of defeating the other.

So far, we have examined multiple aspects related to conflicts between large forces, but what about small ones? How do they play politics? Well, the smallest, or, if you prefer, the weakest, can take advantage of the balance of power within a society. For this, they need only establish friendship with all the divergent stronger members (in the case of countries, we refer to powers) to dominate the point of equilibrium in the balance of power. Securing the friendship of all the stronger members offers the smaller members protection from any aggression. This has been the case in different small countries at different times in history, such as Singapore, Switzerland, or Belgium. Another option that the weakest countries have is to forge close ties to a single power, but this type of relationship reduces their ability to negotiate with regard to the dominant power and puts them at a competitive disadvantage.

So how do small-scale conflicts compare to large-scale ones? The answer is that the same principles apply. We have all seen small political forces prefer to negotiate with more powerful political forces they would have no chance of defeating. Usually, the political forces that face off in a contest are the ones that might be thought to have some chance of beating their rivals. The same holds true for elections within countries, municipalities, and even within small associations such as NGOs.

Economic aspects

As we have already seen, life at all levels is based on competition for resources. It is easy to understand that the concept of unrestricted supply and demand, with its biological and evolutionary underpinnings, is nature itself taken to the economic plane (provided it occurs in conditions of equity). In addition, evidence shows that economic liberalism has been the greatest driver of global economic growth, as Frieden and Lake stated in their book *International Political Economy.* The moments of greatest economic growth in the world have taken place when there was greater freedom to exchange goods as well as peaceful conditions in which to conduct these exchanges. Curiously, these moments of greater economic freedom have taken place under conditions of order imposed by an empire (such as the Roman, British or American).

According to D. Acemoglu and J. Robinson in their book *Why Nations Fail*, the enrichment of a nation lies with order (coinciding with the theory set forth in this book) and equity in relationship to justice institutions. From here, the question arises: How does equity boost the economy? Seen through the lens of the "evolutionary theory of politics", it is not equity that drives the economy but the entire institutional and control system, which is capable of maintaining the necessary order for equity and economic growth to flourish. Without that institutional foundation, any attempt to impose a more equitable society would end up generating another Iraq, another Syria, or another Afghanistan.

It makes sense that communism sold well in the beginning: it offered what was needed for success. Theoretically it implied a greater degree of order, institutional strength, strict compliance with the law, and most certainly, equity among individuals within society. It is easy to visualize it as the system of the future. However, in 1989 the world watched as the socialist empire of the Soviet Union and its satellite countries crumbled. The socialist system had failed irreversibly, giving way to the more open economic system of today's Russia. The capitalists were always arguing that the great weakness of socialism was its lack of incentive to produce, since equality in the distribution of goods demotivated the most hardworking and creative individuals. Perhaps both sides were right in their arguments. It is true that the most orderly human societies reach higher levels of complexity that allow them to be more equitable. However, with no intention of going deeper into the Soviet system, it is striking that a study with Capuchin monkeys at Yale University showed in fact that when a monkey works and notices that his work is not proportional to the benefit received, he stops working.[162] If communism (or socialism, if you prefer to call it that) can be considered the ideal system, it is also true that it ignores some important aspects of our biological, evolutionary and social nature.

I witnessed an example of an international thrashing in my own country during the media attack on

---

162   Fisher, Daniel. n.d. "Primate Economics." Forbes. https://www.forbes.com/2006/02/11/monkey-economics-money_cz_df_money06_0214monkeys.html.

the "Panama Papers" in April 2016. Panama, I dare say, is one of the most capitalist countries in the world. The freedom that it has traditionally offered is reflected in its economic prosperity over the past few years. In fact, for many Panamanians, economic freedom is a good which must continue to be perfected to sustain economic growth in the long term. However, recent difficulties in the world economy have produced all kinds of theorists with magical solutions among which, unquestionably, are those who advocate greater state control of economic growth (collect more taxes to invest more in public services). This last group was able to coordinate a media attack that left this small Central American nation looking like the primate that harms everyone else in the group. A whole community of powers managed to get its citizens to believe that their economies do not grow because of a small developing country. It takes all sorts, as they say, as well as topics that escape the central theme of this book. So, let's leave the thrashing for another book and talk instead about spheres.

Nothing but a bunch of spheres

The sphere, say students of geometry in nature, is the geometric shape with the smallest surface for a given volume. It is seen in planets, stars, bubbles, atoms, etc. Anyway... there are apparently multiple physical reasons that favor the sphere as one of the most common forms in nature.

Perhaps we have never stopped to ask ourselves what relationship this geometric form could possibly have to human congregations. Human clusters do not seem to be exempt from the equivalent of "surface tension", which causes gas bubbles to take the spherical shape that holds the gas molecules together, enabling them to resist the pressure exerted by the surrounding liquid.

Physically, human clusters tend to adopt a spherical shape. This can be seen on any map, where you can observe cities without the geographical features that deform them. You may argue that this is not an example of a sphere but of a flat circle, and you would be correct. Just remember that the ground presents physical resistance to population growth, just as gravity resists vertical growth (even so, it is not uncommon to see the tallest buildings in the center of cities).

It is not only physical distribution that seems to be dominated by spheres; we can also observe that same form dominating social distribution. At some point, we have all heard talk of "social spheres."

Let's take a moment to analyze this. In the end, human societies are natural groupings. Make no mistake, we are animals. It is true that we are more complex because of our greater intelligence, but our societies are living beings and behave as such. We are part of nature. Like every growing being, human societies will begin in a spherical and non-pyramidal way. How so? Well, resources will be concentrated at the center. Immediately surrounding these resources will be the first sphere corresponding to the elites, who will occupy the largest possible volume with the smallest possible area of contact with the next sphere, which is the intermediate layer. Beyond this lies the largest sphere, with the largest size and smallest possible area of contact with the environment, as well as the least access to resources. My friends of a socialist persuasion will almost certainly tell me that this is not fair, but I tell you that it is the most "natural" and normal distribution. In fact, it is said that the richest people in China are connected to the communist party;[163] Fidel Castro's fortune is estimated at 900 million dollars; [164]Hugo Chavez amassed wealth to the tune of one billion dollars;[165] and Joseph Stalin is estimated to have had a fortune of 5.79 billion dollars (one of the richest men in history). [166]This means that the different political alternatives in a society rarely challenge the concentric sphere arrangement. The only difference is in the forms or rules they propose to include or exclude individuals from the spheres that are closer to the concentration of

163   "Richest in China Are Connected with the Communist Party." 2015. Www.Theepochtimes.Com. October 22, 2015. http://www.theepochtimes.com/n3/1882994-richest-in-china-are-connected-with-the-communist-party/.
164   "Fidel Castro Net Worth 2018: Wiki, Married, Family, Wedding, Salary, Siblings." 2020. Net Worth Post. January 3, 2020. http://celebritynetworth.wiki/fidel-castro-net-worth/.
165   Gye, Hugo. 2013. "Was Chavez Worth over $1bn When He Died? Intelligence Analyst Claims He Amassed Huge Fortune from Country's Oil Wealth." Mail Online. March 7, 2013. http://www.dailymail.co.uk/news/article-2289427/Was-Hugo-Chavez-worth-1bn-died-Claims-amassed-huge-fortune-countrys-oil-wealth.html.
166   "From Joseph Stalin to Bill Gates... 10 of the Richest People Who Have Ever Lived." 2017. The Sun. April 29, 2017. https://www.thesun.co.uk/living/3445713/10-of-the-richest-people-who-have-ever-lived/.

resources. The amount of resources that can permeate from the most central spheres to those farthest out also seems to vary.

And what about the global community? Everything that has been said also applies to the global community, which behaves like an enormous living organism with the same distribution pattern as the smallest human groups. That is why we have rich (central) nations, a closely linked intermediate layer (satellite nations), and nations lagging behind and far removed from resources (peripheral nations).

Speaking more realistically, a society does not depend on a single source of resources. There are different sources, with different dimensions and different values. A certain number of individuals will congregate around each source depending on its characteristics. The various sources are linked, which helps hold the structure together (perhaps if Catalonia were physically closer and interconnected with Madrid it would not be asking for independence). Not surprisingly, then, there is not one but multiple spheres of elites, with individuals or groups sharing a privileged position in more than one sphere.

Everything stated in the previous paragraph suggests that a human society is more easily represented as a molecule and not as a group of concentric spheres.

Globalization

In my university years, I recall participating in multiple protests against the changes that occurred in the 90s because of globalization. I was a tough critic of the imposition of neoliberal models in Latin America.

The middle class of which I am part always saw globalization as something bad. The process has been regarded with frustration in view of the asymmetric growth of wealth and an increasingly disproportionate balance of power between large corporations and workers of every skill level.

Today, however, I have no doubt that vertical authority was necessary. The connections generated by globalization have been enlarging human society, making it more complex in a short time. This move to a higher level of complexity, which involved the proliferation of communications and technology, could only be achieved with firm authority. Today we enjoy the connectivity that social networks and virtual commerce give us only because there was order that allowed institutions to prepare to deal with greater social complexity.

Globalization, together with the expansion of communications, occurred under a rather authoritarian process carried out by the richest countries. The process does not seem to be over. The growing virtual integration between companies, governments, and citizens has been happening by leaps and bounds with increasing speed. Therefore, the United States continues to move in the direction of authoritarianism, as clearly evidenced by the election of President Trump at a time when the complexity of the country's social and economic problems is growing.

China, in contrast, could be on its way to a more egalitarian system in spite of – and at the same time, thanks to - a governance structure that has been able to maintain the order needed for the country to move forward in industry and technology.

In short, globalization has implied a change in the rules of the game, both in politics and in business. An example of this is seen in the fact that in the twentieth century, the elite's access to resources depended heavily on asymmetry in access to information. Today, competition for resources also involves hiding information from cyberspace. While it is true that the asymmetry has been greatly reduced by the dissemination of the internet, it has also become easier to spread false information. As a result, the elite is now integrated by individuals with the ability to access useful and accurate information and integrate it into real knowledge, until it becomes wisdom.

Xenophobia and migration

As we saw before, all social animals have three options for getting closer to the highest quality resources:

1. Adapt to the rules of competition within the group;

4. Migrate to another group in which you can move higher up the social ladder; or

5. Go it alone, in which case you lose all the benefits of life in society.

The tendency of humans, throughout time, has been to migrate. Our brain seems to have developed due to constant and drastic climate changes that forced us to adapt and constantly move in search of resources. Human groups tend to go wherever greater benefits can be obtained, just like the first human groups moved around looking for food to collect and animals to hunt.

An abundance of resources will always attract individuals from other parts. It is in our DNA. For practical purposes, economic growth and high employment are an abundance of resources, offering a better life with the same amount of effort.

Upon arriving at a new destination, migrants will encounter a group already established around available resources. This previously assembled group must now choose between the risk of sharing the resources and the cost of organizing to defend exclusive access to the resources. It is precisely here that populist discourse finds a receptive audience since populism tends to minimize the complexity and potential cost of defending resources.

The new arrivals will invoke the equality of the first human societies of hunter-gatherers, like any human being who feels competitively disadvantaged against the pre-established system. Meanwhile, the group that had previously gathered around the resources will draw on their non-human primate origins to organize hierarchically against what can be interpreted as an external threat.

Clearly, there are multiple angles to the fear of ethnic minorities, among which cultural, economic and political variables can be identified. Each of these variables is present to a different degree in each country and in each context. The future of migration policies will depend on the evolution of cosmopolitan values with respect to globalization, the strength of democratic institutions, the inclusiveness of the political culture, and the ideological legitimacy of political actors[167]. However, it cannot be denied that two key factors in the current migratory dynamics are the availability of employment and economic development.

There are times when immigration can provide valuable labor as well as intellectual capital that help to sustain economic growth and generate more employment. In fact, immigration and economic growth can form a virtuous cycle of economic development.

Migration problems become more prevalent when unemployment increases or there is a slowdown in the economy. A recession can cause migration to be an economic threat with more people competing for increasingly scarce resources. After identifying immigrants as an economic threat, they are branded a cultural or social threat.[168]

Xenophobia is defined as discrimination against foreigners, who are perceived as different from most of the population. While the word xenophobia has a different connotation than racism, the concepts are related and often stem from similar motivations. Racism places a certain racial or religious group in a

---

167   Miller, Jennifer, and Lars Rensmann. n.d. "Xenophobia and Anti-Immigrant Politics." *Oxford Research Encyclopedia of International Studies*. Accessed July 14, 2020.
http://www.academia.edu/3363548/Xenophobia_and_An-
ti-Immigrant_Politics.
168   Cea D'Ancona, Ma *Ángeles. 2015. "Immigration as a Threat: Explaining the Changing Pattern of
Xenophobia in Spain." Journal of International Migration
and Integration* 17 (2): 569–91. https://doi.org/10.1007/
s12134-015-0415-3.

predetermined position of power within society.[169]

The recent difficulties faced by most of the developed countries to boost the growth of their economies has led to the increased popularity of proposals such as the construction of a wall between the United States and Mexico (by President Trump), and the United Kingdom's exit from the European Union. All this suggests that the Holocaust did not occur during the Great Depression by chance. Under conditions of unemployment, immigrants easily become targets of populist politicians and demagogues and can quickly go from being a vulnerable group to being singled out as the main cause of any social problem.

The case of Islamophobia, however, is a bit different. Islamophobia is more easily compared with the Cold War than with mere xenophobia. There are Muslim groups which, like certain political groups in the past, have advocated for ideological expansion without any respect for existing borders. On the one hand, there is discrimination against Muslims, but on the other, attacks motivated by ideological expansion have become highly effective at producing civilian deaths and material damage.

Knowledge, information and communications

Just as the Iron Age ushered in the manufacture of new tools which could later be used as weapons, communications

---

169   "Xenophobia | Encyclopedia.Com." n.d. Www.Ency-clopedia.Com. Accessed July 14, 2020. http://www.encyclo-pedia.com/medicine/psychology/psychology-and-psychia-try/xenophobia.

and information are facilitating the development of new weapons of manipulation and psychological warfare. The opening up of communications and the rise of non-national organizations (commercial, activist, terrorist, religious, ideological, xenophobic, discriminatory, etc.) that transcend borders have allowed the use of communications for a variety of subjects, with a greater geographical range than missiles.

Open communication is far from being the perfect way to access information, since it can also facilitate the dissemination of prejudices, biased interpretations, or fictitious facts. In the end, excessive information, both true and false, can lead the individual to paralysis, which may be manifested as apathy in the face of the different problems that circulate in the information networks.

The use of social networks as a tool for disseminating information that is often biased, prejudiced, or false is forcing the emergence of a culture of information verification.

Although the foundation of democracy is the free exchange of ideas, excessive information and political marketing practices are progressively undermining it. Instead of addressing disputes through a breakdown of arguments and analysis (in a contest to persuade an audience about a cause or the best way to solve problems), the contenders have turned to adopting beliefs and prejudices in order to manipulate the audience in exchange for votes.

The management of information on preferences and marketing garnered through the internet and social networks has opened wide the door for the proliferation of populism on both sides, right and left. In what has become a competition between marketing strategies, votes are sought by repeating what is already known that people want to hear. Arguments to persuade the majority about a certain ideology increasingly lose their validity, and finally, all electoral options end up looking alike.

As a result of this blatant use of marketing tactics, the development of ideological theory and definition has been replaced by political mercantilism for the sole purpose of coming into power. This switchout has been debilitating to governance since it has led governments to strip the ideological platform on which they act. Authorities are running out of tools to solve complex problems, against which cronyism has been gaining the advantage.

So, what does this phenomenon of communications and the proliferation of political marketing signify? Politically, the response has been mixed, and has varied from country to country. Smothered in an avalanche of information, the paralysis of a large part of the population has favored the participation of organized civil society, particularly when it is organized to filter the circulating information. On the other hand, when a group that is organized to apply political pressure grows too much, public opinion reaches a level of such complexity that some governments end up resorting to authoritarianism as a way of maintaining order.

The takeaway is that communications represent a great step forward for democracy, as long as:

1. the population is educated to filter the veracity of the circulating information;

2. civil society is organized to contribute and apply pressure, with professionalism, toward concrete solutions, and does not become a tool for mass mobilization based on emotions;

3. the population is educated to channel their vote to an ideological platform, and not to cronyistic or emotional tactics.

Without a doubt, a professional civil society is a point of reference for public opinion, provided it promotes a virtuous cycle between educating the public and gaining the public's trust in a professional, organized civil society.

Post-truth

Post-truth became the word of the year in 2016, with the election of President Trump in the United States. Post-truth refers to circumstances in which objective facts are less influential than emotions in forging public opinion. In his campaign, Trump appealed to emotions through a variety of means, including fear and anxiety. Among the post-truths deployed in the information battle are falsehoods, half-truths and "alternative truths", all of which appeal to emotions, prejudices, and popular beliefs. Post-truth emerged as a result of the erosion of the arguments presented by the mainstream media and its subsequent loss of credibility. With the election of Trump, it was demonstrated that an eroded media can easily be overwhelmed by social networks. A study by Stanford University found that 80 percent of the participants were not able to distinguish between a news item and an advertisement sent by a friend, meaning that a story posted social media is more likely to be believed even though it has not been verified.[170]

What about alternative truth? Is that possible? Ask any scientist and the answer would be a resounding "no", but in politics, there can be a truth that responds to alternative facts. Seriously? Well, yes. Alternative events are nothing more than distortions of real events, according to the convenience of each of the parties in their information battle to persuade the population.[171] That is, distorted realities which would otherwise be falsehoods are now called alternative facts, which give rise to alternative truths.

Building a political system on truth and not post-truth takes effort in terms of educating and promoting critical thinking in the voting population to reduce contamination in the political arena.

When politicians betray us

Who can understand why a politician would want to betray his constituents, when they depend on public opinion for their livelihood as elected officials?

In reality, the line between those who commit illegal acts and those who do not is a blurry one,

---

170 "From Post-Truth to Post-Lies." n.d. Psychology Today. https://www.psychologytoday.com/blog/intentional-insights/201703/post-truth-post-lies.
171 *The Guardian*. 2017. "'Alternative Facts' – the Greatest, Strongest Facts That Ever Existed," January 23, 2017. https://www.theguardian.com/us-news/shortcuts/2017/jan/23/alternative-facts-the-greatest-strongest-facts-that-ever-existed.

determined by weighing the potential benefits, whether social, moral or economic (usually economic), against the potential cost, which again can be economic, social or moral (more frequently moral). This can be shown as an equation:

$P = B - (S * p)$
P = probability of committing a crime
B = potential benefit
S = severity of potential penalty
p = probability of being sanctioned in the attempt

The perception of moral cost is specific to each individual and will be the decisive factor in this equation. Does that mean that the moral scale varies among individuals, and that those with higher moral standards will be less tempted to commit crimes? Perhaps... but what if we return to the topic of the cerebral amygdala we touched on in chapter VIII? It could simply be that those who are most afraid of receiving a public sanction such as going to jail are the ones who are at least risk of committing acts contrary to the law, and that those who perceive a lower risk of being sanctioned take a more defiant attitude. In fact, it is not uncommon that even in vertical societies led by some iron-fisted dictator, serious street crime may not be a problem but all sorts of pilfering is carried out by the family and those close to the dictator.

In short, there are no treacherous politicians or honest politicians per se. What exists is the risk and severity of potential sanctions. In societies with robust institutions, it is because of the certainty of punishment that politicians do not hesitate to obey the law, or, in the case of Capuchin monkeys, the coins of others are not stolen.

The mix of institutional weakness and certain cultural features, such as the culture of easy money, turn any society into the perfect breeding ground for the proliferation of organized crime and its subsequent penetration into local politics. It can be said that the fight against corruption goes hand in hand with any policy against organized crime.

This is why political debate needs to be elevated to strengthen institutions in the face of growing manipulation of public opinion with a populist bent.

As for political cronyism, it can be understood as a form of corruption. For what reason? Simple: cronyism is nothing more than the attempt to seek reciprocity in what appears to be altruism, but where communal goods are the currency. In the end, a personal benefit is sought (votes), but using the commons of society.

So, we now know what we are, where we came from, how we got to this point, and where "this point" is. But will it always be like this? Will we keep changing? That is what the next chapter is about: predictions and politics in humanity.

X. Predicting politics in human societies

It seems daring to finish a book of literature review and analysis with a chapter on predictions. By predictions, I do not mean that we will go into a trance as we gaze into a crystal ball or sift through tea leaves. Nevertheless, despite the efforts of advocates of political forecasting to turn it into an exact science, it remains an esoteric one. Even with all the current tools, political forecasts often perform no better than the odds favoring a particular winner at the horse races. Predicting political outcomes continues to be about as precise as the lottery or a game of bingo.

The proof of this lies in the fact that there are economic groups that bet billions of dollars on candidates who lose, despite the experts. Similarly, there are thousands of individuals from different interest groups in different democratic cultures who volunteer for days on end to support candidates that have no chance of winning. This can be seen in election after election all over the world.

So, what forecasting tools do we have available? Is it possible to establish mathematical relationships that allow us to predict the behavior of animal societies, including human societies? Yes indeed! There are all kinds of tools: mathematical projections, observations of previous patterns (like those used for economic predictions, which often do not work either), or even game theory can be used. The problem is that the factors that influence individual political behavior are so numerous that it is exceedingly difficult to incorporate them all into a mathematical equation. For a population of millions of inhabitants, the factors are even greater, more complex, and more difficult to quantify in order to plug them into an equation.

For the moment, with the intention of predicting the behavior of animals, critical predictions have been made in zoology. These can be tested with field observations or experiments. It is not easy to test predictions with experiments since they can alter social behavior, necessitating the use of multiple lines of evidence to avoid bias.[172]

We also know that a time model for the development of neurological events in different mammals (including their order and duration) has demonstrated high predictability despite evolutionary changes. The model has been applied for the prediction of human neuronal development and has shown great variability in the development of the primate limbic system which, as

---

172   "Animal Social Behaviour - The How and Why of Social Behaviour." n.d. Encyclopedia Britannica. Accessed July 14, 2020. https://www.britannica.com/topic/animal-social-behaviour/The-how-and-why-of-social-behaviour.

we know, is related to emotions and memory. Despite a good level of predictability, it was found that neural events are more difficult to predict following postnatal development, when behavior-related traits begin to be defined. [173]This is logical, since our neuronal physiology is only one of the aspects that determine our behavior: previous experiences, emotions, everything plays a role when adopting a certain behavior.

It should be mentioned that despite the difficulties and inaccuracies inherent to political forecasting, a group of researchers found that among cellphone users, mobility is highly predictable and regular in most individuals regardless of their differences. This means that the study of patterns can play a key role in traffic engineering, urban planning and epidemiology.[174] It could also mean that while not everything is predictable, certain patterns of social behavior may be.

Considering the above, and pursuant to the examination and review of multiple social events throughout history, I propose the "Evolutionary Theory of Politics". It is the product of the observation of a repetitive pattern between hierarchical verticalization to maintain social order, and social egalitarianism. It seems that social changes due to advances in

---

173   Clancy, Barbara, Richard B. Darlington, and Barbara L. Finlay. 2000. "The Course of Human Events: Predicting the Timing of Primate Neural Development." *Developmental Science* 3 (1): 57–66. https://doi.org/10.1111/1467-7687.00100.

174   "Human Behavior Is 93 Percent Predictable, Research Shows." n.d. Phys.Org. https://phys.org/news/2010-02-human-behavior-percent.html.

technological complexity make human societies rotate in a helical manner.

The growing interrelationship between economy, society, and political systems has turned human civilization into a complex system in and of itself, with a level of complexity that is increasing rapidly. "Complexity" in this instance is defined as the ability of a system to deal with the changes that are occurring. That complexity continues to increase and will determine many aspects of human existence in the future. In recent years, human civilization has rapidly become a single global system where environmental demands on a group of organisms create the need for more complex behaviors. In this way, we see that on the one hand, as the complexity of the system increases, it encounters barriers in the form of hierarchical structures that subsequently give way to lateral interactions (egalitarianism). On the other hand, when hierarchies are overcome by complexity (in egalitarian systems), they can become process controllers instead of production controllers (hierarchical horizontalization). An example of such hierarchical changes due to an increase in complexity can be seen in corporations in which the decisions have been handed over to teams created for this purpose, to keep from depending on hierarchical control and its limitations.[175]

---

175   Complexity Rising: From Human Beings to Human Civilization, a Complexity Profile — New England Complex Systems Institute. 2014. "New England Complex Systems Institute." New England Complex Systems Institute. 2014. https://necsi.edu/complexity-rising-from-human-be-ings-to-human-civilization-a-complexity-profile.

We can say that a strong authority represents an advantage in moving toward greater complexity considering the resistance that previous barriers in the hierarchical structure represent. With it, the order necessary for a social restructuring is guaranteed according to the needs demanded by the new level of complexity.

While I am in no way attempting to justify authoritarianism as a form of progress, order and compliance with the law are indispensable. Authoritarianism can also be the product of other social phenomena. For example, support for a strong leader of the alpha male variety has been linked to a group's sense of threat or vulnerability. In this way, the perception of racial and economic vulnerability in young Americans seems to have played a role in skewing their preferences in favor of Donald Trump.[176]

We also know that there are situations in which the most vulnerable groups look for someone to defend them. Interestingly, their inclination to support a powerful group or candidate capable of challenging the elite stems from their awareness that they have no chance of winning on their own. In these cases, game theory can be applied to predict the behavior of the social group.

Based on the above, we can say that a human group will organize its social power structure to favor

176   Beauchamp, Zack. 2018. "Study: Obama Voters Switched to Trump Because of Race." Vox. Vox. October 16, 2018. https://www.vox.com/policy-and-politics/2018/10/16/17980820/trump-obama-2016-race-racism-class-economy-2018-midterm.

one side of the scale or the other: authoritarianism or egalitarianism. Basically, the equilibrium point is determined depending on the external threats identified by the members of a society and the level of abuse or damage that the political elite can inflict on the society. The size of the social group and the complexity required for it to function will also influence this balance. The group may be inclined, in the style of primates, to support a strong leader if he is able to maintain order, since evolutionarily speaking, it is preferable to save social resources by avoiding internal conflicts and unrestrained power struggles.

Social change

It would not be out of place to compare the appearance of the printing press with the diffusion of the internet, followed by social networks. It is expected that social networks will increasingly find ways to challenge the "establishment", as in the case of "Brexit". The management of social networks is intertwined with access to the press, with the associated readjustment in the balance of powers that this represents.

The fourth industrial revolution will undoubtedly connect many more people, drastically affecting the way work is performed in companies and factories. While the changes brought about by this revolution may generate unemployment and strong resistance on the part of workers,[177] the drawbacks will be minimal compared

---

177   Marr, Bernard. 2016. "Why Everyone Must Get Ready For The 4th Industrial Revolution." *Forbes*, April 6, 2016. https://www.forbes.com/sites/bernard-

to the benefits in terms of the increased efficiency and effectiveness brought to all activities. Nevertheless, such a transition will require adequate government regulation to ensure security and must consider the unemployment that internet-linked automation will generate.

We are already getting a taste of the changes that await us soon. Everything indicates that children and young people will need to learn to manage access to information, and to discern and select information based on personal and collective goals. It is, in other words, an art form that we will have to nurture.

Trends and behavior

The economy, migratory movement, the flow of the masses and urban crime all have a common denominator in the influence of the media and the emergence of a group effect which becomes visible on a large scale. The organization of group patterns can be observed both qualitatively and quantitatively. Usually the patterns first emerge on a small scale among only a few individuals, starting a trend which then grows into what is known as the phenomenon of self-organization.[178]

Such organization and group patterns may serve different purposes, among which criminal acts cannot be ruled out. Human societies are constantly generating

---

marr/2016/04/05/why-everyone-must-get-ready-for-4th-in-dustrial-revolution/.

178   "Predicting the Unpredictable – Human Behaviors and Beyond | Mathematics of Planet Earth." n.d. Accessed July 14, 2020. http://mpe.dimacs.rutgers.edu/2013/06/28/ predicting-the-unpredictable-human-behaviors-and-be-yond/.

individuals with antisocial behaviors as well as groups of malcontents. It seems that one of the noble tasks of social institutions is to prevent these individuals from going over the rest of us to gain access to power.

In humans, collective behavior as a form of group reaction often occurs in violation of laws, institutions and social norms, with participants even resorting resort to violence, destruction, or other forms of anarchy. Collective behavior reactions are usually guided by group dynamics in which individuals are encouraged to take actions that would often be unthinkable under normal conditions. It has been proposed that one actor can create an interpretation of the acts of another social actor, and that the so-called "forces" are nothing more than the product of a social argument based on such "interpretation." Four forms of collective behavior have been proposed:

- the crowd, which implies a gathering of people that can become irrational;

- the public, which, unlike the crowd, is focused on a single issue under discussion;

- the mass, which, unlike the public and the crowd, is guided by a group that can involve media or social networks; and

- the social movement, which begins as collective behavior but ends up establishing firm institutional changes.

Collective behaviors develop from the contagion of a behavior within a group and the convergence of individuals who wish to engage in this behavior. They occur because of a norm that emerges at a specific moment in time, as an escape valve to release collective stress.

Of course, all four collective behaviors - the crowd, the public, the mass, and the social movement – are strengthened under conditions of better and more efficient forms of communication, including social networks. This communication advantage will certainly favor any social movement seeking to challenge the political "status quo", a fact which governments and politicians are perfectly aware of and one of the drivers of cyber espionage and the use of trolls (fake virtual accounts used for emotional manipulation). At present, political muscle relies heavily on the virtual world, a phenomenon that will probably only continue to increase in the coming years. The big challenge throughout the world seems to be to get the crowd to take to the streets to exert pressure. Surely, the fourth industrial revolution will be able to better link face-to-face pressure with virtual pressure.

Our brain and the meaning of things

It seems there are issues on which there will never be a consensus, such as sexuality, gender, migration, security, terrorism, etc. The simple explanation for this is that even though we are using the same words, the meaning that our brain gives them is affected by the set of beliefs held by each individual.[179] The issues that

---

179   Li, Ping, Benjamin Schloss, and D. Jake Follmer. 2017. "Speaking Two 'Languages' in America: A Semantic Space Analysis of How Presidential Candidates and Their

divide society can be interpreted in two or more ways, leading to sterile exchanges of opinion using the same terms but with different meanings.

To this day, we continue to debate the impact and influence of different aspects of our surroundings on human perception. Students of the subject have tried to classify our actions and behaviors into those that are learned and those that are the product of interaction with the environment, but results seem to indicate that the two are inseparable. Studies in newborns reveal that the proportion of learned versus unlearned traits depends entirely on the neurological maturity of the newborn.

This leads us to believe that politics continues to be an art form, since it depends on the extreme complexity of the human brain, constant social change, and the complexity of the interactions between human groups. All of which means that we are still far from being able to predict the political behavior of a group fully and accurately.

Despite the complexities, there are well-described forms of interaction between the environment and our brain. An example is the left brain's difficulty in processing changes in the environment and the need to reduce the problem to a pre-determined approach.[180] In fact, this form of interaction can predispose individuals

Supporters Represent Abstract Political Concepts Different-ly." *Behavior Research Methods* 49 (5): 1668–85. https://doi.org/10.3758/s13428-017-0931-5.

180   Cozolino, Lou. 2018. "Conservative Brains vs Liberal Brains | The Science of Psychotherapy." The Science of Psychotherapy. August 6, 2018. https://www.thescienceof-psychotherapy.com/conservative-brains-vs-liberal-brains/.

with greater development in the left hemisphere to be more vulnerable to populist discourse in which complex problems are reduced to a childlike level of simplicity.

The reason behind this kind of interaction is the fact that in humans, the brain is the organ that consumes the most energy. Representing only 2% of total body weight, it consumes 20% of the body's energy[181].[182] However, its operation is highly efficient, so much so that it was estimated to be 100,000 times more efficient in its energy consumption than a computer in 2012.[183] This efficiency is important, especially for computer engineers and evolutionary biologists. It is also becoming increasingly important for politicians.

It has been shown that when more demanding mental tasks are performed, there is a greater consumption of glucose by the brain cells. A shortage of this sugar manifests as mental exhaustion. This occurs particularly with mental effort that does not generate any satisfaction or pleasure, so humans tend to reject intellectual challenges with changes in emotions. It is

181   Harmon, Katherine. n.d. "Earlier Model of Human Brain's Energy Usage Underestimated Its Efficiency." Scientific American. Accessed July 14, 2020. https://www.scientificamerican.com/article/brain-energy-efficiency/.
182   "The Brain – Our Most Energy-Consuming Organ." n.d. University World News. Accessed July 14, 2020. http://www.universityworldnews.com/article.php?story=20130509171737492.
183   Abate, Tom. 2014. "Stanford Bioengineers Create Circuit Board Modeled on the Human Brain." Stanford University. April 28, 2014. https://news.stanford.edu/news/2014/april/neurogrid-boahen-engineering-042814.html.

thought that the brain even promotes chemical states to avoid prolonged and strenuous concentration.[184] These biological facts can make people prefer simplistic and populist speeches.

To put it simply, we can say that if increased complexity is going to lead to a change in the discourse, the change will be to present the problems in simpler terms. In this context, the advance in populism seems inevitable in future political contests throughout the world. Social complexity is exceeding the individual capacity of our brains, progressing faster than our own natural biological evolution, and this changes all the rules of the game in communications with the public. The mass will become increasingly more dependent on opinion leaders, meaning that any race for power must necessarily focus on gaining the confidence of the voters.

Exercising politics

The eternal struggle for power, with marketing tools as the main weapon in democracy, leads to a style of politicians with increasingly short-term appeal, while the new generations are becoming more and more used to obtaining instant results at the speed of an Internet search. Remember that our cousins, the apes, have no sense of long-term reward, which suggests that deep within human nature, the concept of sacrifice in exchange for almost immediate benefits prevails.

---

184   Jabr, Ferris. n.d. "Does Thinking Really Hard Burn More Calories?" Scientific American. Accessed July 14, 2020. https://www.scientificamerican.com/article/thinking-hard-calories/.

In social and political systems, governments face the dilemma of how to deal with complex situations: the right way, or the "politically correct" way. While it is true that the majority is usually silent in a democracy, there are always participatory voices. The right way and the "politically correct" way draw closer together as civil society becomes more organized and involved at its different levels within the system. High-level debates, mutual trust between governments and civil society, and consistency between words and actions: these are some of the elements that can facilitate the formulation of strategic actions by governments. In the end, the involvement of society in decisions leads to more correct decisions in the medium term. In contrast, the less participatory a society is in the national or local debate, the more vulnerable a country will be to populism. And in countries with weak institutions, populism can facilitate corruption and political patronage.

Populism is more about rhetoric than ideology. It promotes positions that lead human psychology to view complex issues as a battle between good and evil, offering simple answers to intricate problems. Usually populism is sold as anti-elitism. Populism is widely practiced today, but little known as a concept. It involves a charismatic leader who supports the views of the general population on issues that arouse concern, fear and passion. There are moderate forms of populism limited to choosing the most widespread and supported position among voters (often seen in political marketing). Populist leaders commonly make promises that cannot be fulfilled, seemingly ignoring the potential consequences if they are elected. The most common populist right-wing arguments in recent years have focused on anxiety about the economy, immigration and sexual and reproductive rights (the latter being a special favorite of religious control groups), while left-wing populists have maintained the discourse of class struggle and resentment towards economic groups.

Political clientelism, on the other hand, offers political support during a campaign in exchange for certain benefits, such as gifts to voters or jobs to those who help campaign. Political clientelism leads to clear inefficiencies and misuse of funds in any government system, exacerbating social inequities.[185]

Among the forms of clientelism is *paternalism,* in which the costs associated with a presumably vulnerable group are transferred to other groups deemed less vulnerable. Paternalism is mentioned here as a form of clientelism because the benefits received by the more vulnerable group translate into votes for the candidate whose political positions favor them. Clientelism and paternalism garner short-term popular support, helping to perpetuate inequality in systems with anemic control institutions through the near-sighted decisions of their political class. Importantly, the paternalized group gives up not only its freedom but its opportunities, since paternalism does not promote the medium- and long-term decision making that would provide vulnerable groups with better opportunities and make for a more

185   Robinson, James A., and Thierry Verdier. 2013. "The Political Economy of Clientelism*." *The Scandinavian Journal of Economics* 115 (2): 260–91. https://doi.org/10.1111/sjoe.12010.

equitable society.[186]

Finally, looking ahead, it would not be unthinkable to visualize the consolidation of technocratic authoritarianism by intergovernmental agencies to pressure governments to execute necessary changes. We are going to see this phenomenon more and more often in developing countries. Similarly, soon we will see increasingly robust international organizations - backed by intergovernmental agencies - with the mission of strengthening civil societies in countries with weak institutions.

Future of the process

It is not surprising that short periods of authoritarianism have marked the global integration process to maintain order in the face of increasing social complexity. After each period of authoritarianism, a process of struggle for equity between nations is also to be expected; it is as simple as seeing all nations as a community of living beings. The system of international law that governs humanity has not taken this into account, since each country represents a single vote and any distortion in the balance of power can be attributed to a country's purchasing power or military capacity. However, a readjustment in the weight of each country based on the size of its population is likely to occur.

---

186   Marzonetto, Gabriela. n.d. "Clientelism and Paternalism in Politics: Undemocratic Institutions That Emerge after Financial and Economic Crises." *Www.Academia. Edu.* Accessed July 14, 2020. https://www.academia. edu/5871895/Clientelism_and_Paternalism_in_Politics_Undemocratic_institutions_tha

While it is true that the information age can lead to a more equitable society provided there are strong institutions, it is also true that the easy dissemination of information can lead to social collapse in the style of the Soviet Union if used predominantly to disrupt the traditional order.

Clearly, information plays a key role in the distribution of social power. If the distribution of information changes, there may be a readjustment in the makeup of the elite. It is known that the expansion of the elite class usually produces instability, division and conflict within human societies; the same holds true for communities of countries. Presently, we can observe how traditional European powers are coming up against large emerging countries with great potential, leaving them no choice but to accept these newcomers into the elite and grant them a relevant position proportional to their economic capacity and increasing military might. This can produce destabilization and the formation of new alliances that can lead to new wars. Now, the big question is, will wars continue to be violent? It is hard to say, but other forms of war can certainly be observed (commercial, monetary, etc.) that have been played for decades and may be a less harmful way to sublimate conflicts of interest between blocks.

Additionally, the dissemination in cyber-space of religious and philosophical ideas that feed on prejudices is becoming a genuine threat, since it violates the sovereignty of other states and can spread ideas contrary to the needs of each country, affecting their governance.

One topic that is subject to constant speculation concerns the future of terrorism; therefore, this chapter would not be complete without a discussion of the Islamic State. Isis, like the other groups of the Muslim brotherhood (Iran, Hamas, Hezbollah, Al-Qaeda, etc.), will continue to challenge international borders with the goal of establishing a global caliphate. If no agreement exists between the powers to set limits on their expansionist ideology, the number of victims will continue to grow, just as it would have in Nazi Germany if World War II had not exploded.

Historically, expansionist ideologies (Hitler, Napoleon, etc.) have spurred the unity of peoples threatened by disrespect for their borders. In the Middle East, however, consensus cannot be achieved due to the radicalization of points of view and differences in the philosophical concepts themselves (remember that the same word can have more than one meaning for the human brain, depending on the development of its different areas, emotions, previous experiences, etc.), including concepts around humanity, religion, international relations and others. The region is expected to remain in conflict until such time as Russia, the United States, China and the other powers that influence the region achieve their own consensus regarding their interests. Only an alliance with sufficient military and economic capacity can impose an order that would prevent sectarian struggles. Once a sustainable order is established and sufficient institutional maturity is achieved, the implementation of a more equitable system can be reconsidered. Any attempt to implement an equitable system at this time would only result in a bloodbath due to further sectarian confrontations.

Climate change

Today, it is unlikely that anyone still has doubts about the role that climate change will play in the future of power dynamics.

Violent climatic changes have been the driver of our natural selection as the dominant species and have accompanied us throughout our most important achievements as societies.

Climate change seems inevitable with or without our presence on the planet and introduces factors that challenge our ability to control the situation through technology. For this reason, I don't see a future for the environmental movement that is trying to prevent climate change. This does not mean that I am not in favor of conserving nature, lowering carbon emissions, or reducing the use of plastics. I simply believe that this is not the future of the political debate on the subject.

Likely, the political debate will polarize between a movement grounded in collective fear that advocates for strong leadership to drive the technology that will enable our social readaptation in the face of climate change. On the other hand, will be a more liberal leadership that promotes behavioral changes within society to promote its adaptation to ongoing changes.

Definitely, to which side the scale tilts will depend on the severity of the changes and how out of control they are perceived to be by the majority.

XI. Recap

Without a doubt, human beings are part of nature. Under no circumstances do we escape the laws that govern the rest of living beings.

The study of primates is a tool that provides vast knowledge about our origins and our nature as a species. And while the science of primatology is barely taking its first steps, it has incalculable potential. However, to realize that potential and continue gathering information about our origins requires the preservation of primate ecosystems.

Our nature will always lead us to compete for more resources. That is, to change "from primates to politicians" as part of our survival instinct. That fight is part of our day-to-day and makes us a true political animal. Not in the sense that Aristotle contemplated, but in the sense of a competition for power in which the only ethical principle that seems to be universal is the need for certainty of punishment.

Such certainty of punishment is not the responsibility of governments alone: society is called to demand justice, to pave conditions that allow fair and equitable competition.

Corrupt politicians, clientelists, despots, populists and other subgenres: these are not who betrays us. Society betrays itself, every time it allows the ascent of a leader without the right profile to provide adequate social governance. We betray ourselves as individuals and as a society every time we expect "someone else" to take control of the situation, or every time we turn a blind eye to the rants of the current heads of state.

The struggle for power, together with the lack of organization in a given society, has allowed different governments throughout the world to be overtaken by bona fide organized crime gangs populated by politicians, bankers, trade unionists, businessmen, and even drug traffickers and money launderers (among others). That rotten core will not change without an open challenge to the dominant elites that can only be achieved through adequate organization and professionalization of the protests of the people.

The virtuous cycle between our intelligence and social complexity has led us to technological advances that have reflected on our social nature. All of these changes - controlling fire, forging iron, agriculture, machines, electricity, computers, telecommunications, and the fourth industrial revolution - have put stress on us as a species, with advances that are coming faster than our capacity for genetic-biological adaptation. They have forced the group of equality-minded hunter-gatherers to return to their origins and behave, at times, like their cousins the primates.

The "evolutionary theory of politics" developed in this book explains the oscillations in leadership styles throughout history. Cycles of authoritarianism alternated with equity seem to be the natural response of the societies created by our species, in the face of the stress that our own technological advances represent.

Regarding the inevitable question of whether liberals or conservatives do a better job of governing, we could say that both ideologies are necessary, that rotation in power is good, and that the clear ideological definition of political currents enriches democracy. The balance between conservatives and liberals prevents liberals from making changes so fast that things get out of hand and end up in anarchy similar to the French revolution, just as it prevents conservatives from establishing a kind of monarchy that would return us to the obscurantism of the Middle Ages. Social progress depends on both ideologies for changes to take place gradually, at a speed that allows their assimilation by the majority in an atmosphere of social organization, without leading to chaos.

I want to end by thanking you for the time you have taken to read this entire analysis. There is no doubt that our brain is complex, as is our biology. Our societies are even more complex since they are the result of the interaction between our biological characteristics and the evolution of the brain of the most intelligent animal on the planet.

But no matter how intelligent, sophisticated and complex we become, our ancestors will always be hanging around backstage in our DNA. Our politicians will always be primates, and primates will always be politicians.

About the Author

Juan Manuel Muñoz, born in Panama City, is a physician, political scientist, futurist, business administrator, musician, and social activist in the areas human rights, pacifism, and a movement toward a sustainable environment. He began his participation as social activist during his medical studies at the University of Panama, which led him to sit on the executive board of the International Federation of Medical Students Associations (IFMSA). The current political uncertainty, along with fast-paced political changes, led Muñoz to publish multiple opinion articles in local newspapers, and finally to write *From Primates to Politicians*.

www.ingramcontent.com/pod-product-compliance
Lightning Source LLC
Chambersburg PA
CBHW031509270326
41930CB00006B/321